"Simply an outstanding book. Ni[  ]
in the ancient Roman world and i[  ] ...und practices that made the earliest Christians stand out in contrast.
It left me considering how the church today might recapture
some of the weirdness and beauty that made such a mark on
the ancient world. If you've ever wondered how a tiny Jewish sect, worshiping a crucified Messiah, could ever turn the
Roman Empire upside down, then this book is for you."

—**Mike Erre**, teaching pastor, Journey Church;
host of the *Voxology Podcast*

"For those interested in the historical, social, and religious
setting of the first Jesus-followers, Nijay's book provides a fascinating picture of the many ways in which Christians were
radically different from the people around them. Without
idealizing the church, he demonstrates how their ideas and
practices would have been weird, dangerous, and compelling in their own society. These Christians embodied their
faith within a loving extended family around a God who had
come to earth in Jesus to bring them into an intimate, loving,
Spirit-filled relationship with himself. Here, Nijay explores the
implications of this alien but attractive message."

—**Lucy Peppiatt**, principal, Westminster Theological Centre

"A winsome and accessible introduction to two strange phe-
nomena—the practice of religion in the Greco-Roman world
and the faith and practice of the early Christians within that
world. The first is probably strange to us, the second strange
both to the Christians' ancient neighbors *and* to us. Nijay's exploration of the early Christians' fundamental convictions and
foundational practices promises to help us rethink our own in
a post-Christendom environment, much to the twenty-first

century church's benefit. His exploration of their strangeness promises to give us permission to follow Jesus more fully where obedience might make us look strange today."

—**David A. deSilva**, Distinguished Professor, Ashland Theological Seminary

"Gupta takes us to the streets of Rome, where gods and their temples stand on just about every corner and where people look to their deities not so much for pardon or ethical transformation as for riches, spells, vendettas, state protection, and victory over enemies. Onto these streets in the first century, Gupta vividly tells us, came the very strange followers of Jesus with their news of a recent crucifixion and resurrection, the renewal of all things, and, above all, a loving Father who is forming a community marked by love amid the evils and anxieties of the world. At a time when contemporary Christians seem uncomfortable appearing odd to their neighbors, Gupta's reminder of the inherent strangeness of the way of Christ is refreshing and vital."

—**John Dickson**, Distinguished Professor, Wheaton College; host of the *Undeceptions* podcast; author of *Bullies and Saints: An Honest Look at the Good and Evil of Christian History*

"An absolute joy to read! It moved not only my mind but also my heart, as I was taken on a fascinating journey into the peculiar lives and beliefs of early Christians. The book is both academically responsible and very practical. It uncovers an example of what it means for Christians to be *in* the world but not *of* the world. Nijay has an uncanny ability to examine ancient texts with precision and care and also to don a pastoral hat to help modern Christians not just study the past but learn from it. Put simply, Nijay's book makes me excited to be a Christian."

—**Preston Sprinkle**, bestselling author and host of the *Theology in the Raw* podcast

"If you have ever asked yourself the question of how others in the ancient world viewed the earliest Christians, then this book is for you! The book highlights how 'weird' the earliest Christians seemed to their neighbors both in their emphasis on belief and in their worship and everyday lives. In the twenty-first century, when Christianity has been so dominant for so long, it is hard to imagine a context in which the Christian faith was viewed as out of the ordinary and in some respects dangerously weird. This book may be short, but it packs a punch and is well worth reading."

—**Paula Gooder**, canon chancellor, St. Paul's Cathedral, London

"A must-read for anyone seeking a deeper understanding of the cultural context of the New Testament. I wholeheartedly endorse *Strange Religion* as an essential addition to your reading list. You'll love it."

—**Kat Armstrong**, Bible teacher and author of the Storyline Project Bible study series

"Gupta attempts to explain how what is familiar to us, Christianity, appeared to be a dangerous and strange superstition in the Greco-Roman world. Whether it is religion without a temple and sacrifices, believing in belief, the ethics of equality, or even hopes for an embodied afterlife, Gupta shows just how 'weird' Christians seemed to their contemporaries in antiquity. A terrific resource for anyone wanting to enter the world of the first Christians and understand how Christians were once loathed for practicing a rogue religion."

—**Michael F. Bird**, deputy principal, Ridley College, Melbourne, Australia

"Gupta matches his impeccable New Testament research with a sensitive eye toward the work of the Spirit for the twenty-first century church. This book is insightful, funny, captivating, and forceful all at once. More than anything, *Strange Religion* reminds the church of its mission: keep things weird."

—**A. J. Swoboda**, associate professor, Bushnell University; author of *After Doubt*

# Strange Religion

*How the First Christians Were Weird,*
*Dangerous, and Compelling*

# NIJAY K. GUPTA

**BrazosPress**

*a division of Baker Publishing Group*
Grand Rapids, Michigan

© 2024 by Nijay K. Gupta

Published by Brazos Press
a division of Baker Publishing Group
Grand Rapids, Michigan
www.brazospress.com

Printed in the United States of America

Library of Congress Cataloging-in-Publication Data
Names: Gupta, Nijay K., author.
Title: Strange religion : how the first Christians were weird, dangerous, and compelling / Nijay K. Gupta.
Description: Grand Rapids, Michigan : Brazos Press, a division of Baker Publishing Group, [2024] | Includes bibliographical references.
Identifiers: LCCN 2023027170 | ISBN 9781587435171 (paperback) | ISBN 9781587436260 | ISBN 9781493444922 (ebook) | ISBN 9781493444939 (pdf)
Subjects: LCSH: Church history—Primitive and early church, ca. 30–600. | Christian sociology—History—Early church, ca. 30–600.
Classification: LCC BR162.3 .G856 2024 | DDC 270.1—dc23/eng/20231018
LC record available at https://lccn.loc.gov/2023027170

Baker Publishing Group publications use paper produced from sustainable forestry practices and post-consumer waste whenever possible.

24  25  26  27  28  29  30      7  6  5  4  3  2

To A. J., John, and Morris

# Contents

# Preface

This book started with a question someone asked during one of my lectures: "Why did the early Christians call themselves 'believers'?" Someone else raised a related question: "Did other religious groups at this time call themselves 'believers'?" That led me down a path of research that became this book. Not only could I not find another group that talked about themselves like this, but I found that ancient people rarely used the language of "belief" for religion. I concluded that Christians were weird. *Were they weird in other ways?* I wondered. I set out to spend a few years studying ancient religions in general and Roman religion in particular, and I came to a clear conclusion: by and large, early Christians were weird and were dangerous to many, and yet clearly some found this religion attractive and compelling.

This book is not a handbook for how to be Christian today or how to create a "weird" church. Largely, I see the work I have done as descriptive—these are the first Christians, warts and all. They were not bucking conventions and pop religion to be special or different. In their best and most genuine moments, they were simply following Jesus, like mice blindly chasing after the pied piper. As they did so, they deviated from the norm of religion, and, whether they were intending to or not, they stood out in society. This deviation from the norm is one way of defining what it means to be "weird." Another way is simply to say that "weird" things belong in another category. I am hoping that an extended investigation of the beliefs, practices, and ethos of the early Christians will clarify their origins and foundations, and provide insight into authentic Christianity today.

Special thanks to my editor, Bryan Dyer, and the conversations that came out of Ambrose University's Downey Lectures and Abilene Christian University's Carmichael-Walling Lectures that I gave on this topic. Also, I taught a doctoral seminar at Northern Seminary in 2021 comparing early Christianity and Greco-Roman religion. I gained so much from these students, especially their presentations on Greco-Roman religion.

I dedicate this book to the rich community of ministry leaders in Portland, Oregon, who graciously live the gospel of Jesus Christ, especially my friends A. J., John, and Morris.

# Introduction

## Keep It Weird

I live in Portland, Oregon, the "weird" capital of the United States. Portlanders are suspicious of anything that smacks of low-quality, mass-production consumerism. "Conformity" is a four-letter word. On an iconic wall downtown our civic motto is inscribed for all to see: "Keep Portland Weird." (A local resident called the "unipiper" is known to ride in circles on a unicycle in front of this sign, wearing a Darth Vader mask and playing bagpipes that blow blasts of fire. Google it.) And by and large Portlanders don't like religion, especially organized religion, and *especially* Christianity. Portland fancies itself an intellectual community that values science and logic, not superstition and "red state" religion. To put it another way, the people who live around me see American Christianity as the *opposite of weird*. It's normal, so normal it's sickening. It adds nothing to society except a vestige of America's racist, sexist, exclusionist past. And sometimes when I go to church here (or elsewhere in America), I can see some of what they mean. Church can easily become just one more thing on a to-do list for the week, and one thing that can be skipped

easily, because it's just another place to consume content and reinforce wider cultural values. And, even worse, church can showcase and promote some of American culture's darkest vices: exploitation, greed, narcissism, extreme individualism, sexism, classism, nationalism, and racism.

I have had countless conversations with pastors about how church life got upended during the 2020 lockdown, attendance dwindled during the online church era of 2020–21, and then when things started to open up again, people just didn't come back. They learned to live without church, and then they realized that they could live without church. So they did. Church was too normal. It competed with everything else going on, so it faded into the background of their lives. Sure, every now and again there was a twinge of nostalgia mixed with guilt, a little nag that said, "Maybe you should go back." But for many that minor pang was not enough to inspire them to get up and go out.

I'm not against tradition. I like routine, and I like many "normal" things. I am a creature of habit. So, I am not going to talk about how churches need to be spontaneous and constantly "shake things up." *But* as a historian and New Testament scholar, I am struck by the contrast between modern American Christianity (often viewed as a mirror of the worst of culture) and the Jesus communities of the first century. When it comes to the churches associated with the apostle Paul, you couldn't imagine a more opposite scenario! *The first Christians were weird!* There's no denying that. I am not talking about their clothing, music preferences, or hobbies. When I say "weird" or "strange," I am talking about deviation from cultural norms and society's expectations for how things ought to be done. Especially when it came to religion—and keep in mind, *everyone* was religious (more on that later)—the Christians were as backwards and as odd as you could be. Now, sometimes Christian writers are accused of exaggerating the uniqueness of Jesus and the apostolic teachings. I am not trying to do that. I don't think the early Christians were perfect or completely alien to their social and cultural world. But there were certain fundamentals of religion that the Christians just didn't have—for example, material sacrifices, physical temples, and formal priests. Such things were the building blocks of religion in the first century, and if you showed up to a Christian gathering in Ephesus or Philippi, you wouldn't find any of these things. Isn't that weird? How is that possible?

I should say from the outset that I don't think the first Christians were *trying* to be weird in order to be weird. They weren't anti-conformist as some sort of intentional political or cultural ideology. In fact, as much as possible, they wanted to prove themselves to be respectable, "good" society members. It was more the case that the person of Christ, the work of the Spirit, and the fundamental dynamics of the gospel themselves changed their orientation toward God, God's world, God's creatures, and God's good end. That made Christians seem like aliens from another planet. They had unusual ways of talking about the divine and about spiritual matters, odd patterns and practices of worship, and suspicious social habits and behaviors. Weird is not always bad (that's why I live in Portland); weird can be good. But weird can also be dangerous. Ideas and persons and institutions that threaten our core values make us nervous. This book is about how earliest Christianity emerged as a new and strange religion that had various effects on people: some were puzzled and others were offended. For example, a second-century opponent of Christianity named Celsus supposedly said, "If all men wanted to be Christians, the Christians would no longer want them."* Some, like Celsus, saw the Jesus people as a plague on society. But some found deep love in the gospel and a new way to live. Say what you will about first-century Christianity, but it was anything but dull and boring.

### Real Coconut Water Is Pink?

I'm one of those weird Portland hippies who likes coconut water. It sounds natural and healthy, and I like eating coconut, so what's not to like? It took me a while to find the coconut water brand that had the right amount of sugar and the right taste for my palate, but it came to be one of my favorite drinks. One day, I was at Costco and I saw a new brand: Harmless Harvest Organic Coconut Water. I liked the idea of buying in bulk at a cheap price, so I picked one up to check it out. *Why is the coconut water pink?* I wondered. I thought maybe I picked up a bad pack, so I looked at another set—*also pink*. In fact, all the packs had pink liquid in the bottles. Lo and behold, there was an explanation on the box under the heading "Naturally Pink." Long story short, when the natural

---

*Contra Celsum 3.9 (trans. Francis Martin, ed., Acts, Ancient Christian Commentary on Scripture, vol. 5 [Downers Grove, IL: InterVarsity, 2006], 180). Here is Miroslav Volf's paraphrase of Celsus: "Christians were so fascinated with rejecting what is common to all people that they themselves would no longer want to be Christians if everyone decided to become one." Volf, Captive to the Word of God (Grand Rapids: Eerdmans, 2010), 75.

coconut sugars touch oxygen, they turn the water pink in only a short time. Pink is what color bottled coconut water *should* be. So why have I only seen clear coconut water before? Many mass-market coconut-water producers use artificial preservatives and other chemicals to maintain a clear and "pristine" appearance. They know that consumers associate "clear" with fresh and clean. Ironically, they add chemicals to make it seem more natural. I know it's just a drink, but I felt lied to by the American food industry! If coconut water is supposed to be pink, I want the pink stuff.

You can see where I am going with this. If coconut water is supposed to be pink, and I'm being sold a manufactured version to make me feel better, what else in life is "supposed to be pink"? What about Christianity? I hesitate to sell you on the idea that *Strange Religion* is the only book on the market to tell you the truth about "real Christianity." I'm Portland weird, but I stop short of being a conspiracy theorist. And yet I do think pop Christianity in the Western world often reflects a "chemically altered" version of the Jesus movement that has been manufactured for cheap refreshment. My goal is to go back to the writings of the apostles and other first-century Christian leaders to see what the "natural ingredients" are in their religion, their faith, and their way of being. With my drinks, I don't care what color they are; I just want to know exactly what I am putting in my body. With my faith, I don't care if it looks strange; give it to me the way it was meant to be! I hope that is why you are reading this book, and I hope it is refreshing.

# Becoming
# Christian

# Roman Religion and the *Pax Deorum*

## Keeping Peace with the Gods

> While Paul was waiting for them in Athens, he was deeply distressed to see that the city was full of idols.
>
> St. Luke, Acts 17:16

### A God on Every Corner

Luke tells us that when Paul found himself in Athens, the bustling and prosperous Greek city, he was confronted with idols all around him. Presumably, this means statues and religious objects representing the many gods worshiped by Athenians. If we could step into a Google Street View tour of first-century Athens, what exactly would we see? Towering statues and monuments of the Olympian greats like Zeus, Poseidon (Athens was only ten kilometers from the sea), Apollo, and the patron goddess Athena herself.

But many other figures, gods and demigods, were honored as well, like the Muses, Egyptian deities, and state leaders like the emperor and prominent war heroes. Store shops would have small cult niches.* Passersby might be wearing a piece of jewelry with cultic symbols for luck. Street merchants would be selling all manner of religious knick-knacks for healing, protection, wisdom, blessing, even the prospect of "gettin' lucky." Just about everywhere Paul turned, he was bound to spot representations of a host of divinities.

Nineteenth-century French historian Numa Denis Fustel de Coulanges once said, "There are in Rome more gods than citizens."[1] Fustel de Coulanges probably got this notion from the Roman Pliny the Elder (23–79 CE), who himself commented on the tendency of Greeks and Romans to fabricate new gods to address every desire and need: "There is a greater population of the Celestials than of human beings, since each individual makes a separate god for himself, adopting his own 'Juno' and his own 'Genius.'"[2] Pliny's statement may sound like an exaggeration—could there really be more gods worshiped than humans to worship them? Perhaps it is a bit over the top, but what we *can* count is the number of religious artifacts that have been unearthed. From the city of Roman Pompeii, archaeologists have discovered thousands upon thousands of statues and images of gods and goddesses. Roman

Figure 1.1. Athena column, Academy of Athens
Marytzouda/Wikimedia Commons/CC by SA 4.0

*Scholars use the term "cult" to refer to religious elements and observances. It doesn't necessarily have a bad connotation when used this way; it is synonymous with "religious" or "worship-related."

Figure 1.2. *St. Paul Preaching in Athens,* by George Baxter (ca. 1855)

historian Mary Beard notes that these cult objects outnumber the estimated population of the city.[3] Here's the upshot: you could hardly turn your head in any household room, shop, public building, or park without seeing the face of a god or some trace of worship depicting their importance for religion, politics, culture, war, and entertainment.

It is truly hard for us (modern Westerners) to imagine that world. Yes, we have our statues of Founding Fathers or great thinkers and inventors in our history, but if we want to get close to the quantity of devotional paraphernalia in major ancient cities like Athens and Pompeii, we need to use a different modern comparison—modern sports heroes. In Portland, we have athletic gods like Damian Lillard (Portland Trailblazers), Tobin Heath (Portland Thorns), and Diego Valeri (Portland Timbers). They are on billboards and signs. You will see black, red, and green jerseys on people walking around the city. Sports mottos like #RipCity, #RCTID, and #BAON are inscribed on bumper stickers and car window decals.* On game days, massive crowds in matching clothes and team scarfs are seen parading from their houses and workplaces down to the stadiums and fields. At the game, you hear communal songs, chants, cheers, and celebrations—with delicious food available, of course. Our modern obsession with sports, especially hero figures and expensive, coveted tickets, corresponds remarkably closely to the idol-saturated world of ancient Athens.

There is a major difference, though, between modern sports and ancient religion. Religion wasn't a hobby for "religious people." It wasn't the entertainment industry. Ancient religion played a crucial role in reinforcing power structures in society, from the gods on high down to peasants, slaves, and criminals. Everyone took seriously a world of rulers and those who were ruled. This was true in terms of human power—governors, emperors, local magistrates, and so on. And it was true of a much bigger cosmological political sphere, with supreme deities, middle-level divinities, and demigods. And mortals found their place in the pecking order, hoping to prevent wrath, inspire blessings, and stay in their own lane.

Greeks and Romans didn't have a "Bible" to tell them what to believe about the world of the gods and how they fit into that world. In part, they had their mythology as recorded in Homer's Greek classics, the *Iliad* and the *Odyssey*, and Hesiod's cosmic genealogy called the *Theogony*. The Romans contributed Virgil's *Aeneid* and the accounts in Livy's record of the history of Rome. But Roman public religion was reinforced mostly through public traditions, rituals, and events. Religion,

---

*#RipCity is the nickname for Portland associated with the Portland Trailblazers. RCTID stands for "Rose City [Sports] Till I Die" (Portland is known as "Rose City"). BAON stands for "By Any Other Name" (another rose reference!). This initialism is associated with our women's soccer team, the Portland Thorns.

politics, culture, philosophy, entertainment, duty, honor, work, family, war, life, and death—these were also knotted together like a big ball of rubber bands. Worship of the gods was central to just about every institution and group. Time and place were not divided into secular and sacred. All was dictated and permeated by the presence, will, and power of the gods, though certain times and places could be supercharged with the sacred.

Today, religion is often seen as a personal choice for the sake of individual or communal inspiration. You can "shop" for churches or try a religion out. The religionist is the consumer, and spiritual goods are the product. But for ancients, it was the other way around. The gods were in charge: they deserved respect and honor, or there would be hell to pay (sometimes literally) for the irreverent. We will talk later about how individual preference might look for an ancient Athenian and Ephesian, but the big picture is this: religion was a corporate obligation that was fulfilled to ensure the welfare of the person, family, city, and state.

## Keeping Peace with the Gods

> "The Romans, like the Greeks, accepted the fundamental principle that the gods existed in the world alongside men and strove with them, in a civic context, to bring about the common good."[4]

The Roman statesman Cicero (106–43 BCE) classically described "religion" as *cultus deorum*, meaning "respect for the gods."[5] The gods deserve human devotion and honor, Cicero believed.[6] The gods are like divine magistrates: humans are their subjects, and they hold sway over human lives and destiny.[7] Plautus (254–184 BCE), Roman playwright of many popular ancient comedies, often had his characters voice common sentiments about life under the reign of the gods: "How something turns out is in the hands of the gods," one character confesses.[8] Another character attributes to almighty Jupiter (similar in powers and position to Zeus among the Greeks) power over all lives, control over the hopes and dreams of mortals, and protection from harm.[9]

Homer's *Iliad* reveals the dark reality of fate, gods abounding in power, and humans trapped and beholden to their whims.

> Such is, alas! the gods' severe decree:
> They, only they are blest, and only free.
> Two urns by Jove's high throne have ever stood,
> The source of evil one, and one of good;
> From thence the cup of mortal man he fills,
> Blessings to these, to those distributes ill;
> To most he mingles both: the wretch decreed
> To taste the bad unmix'd, is cursed indeed;
> Pursued by wrongs, by meagre famine driven,
> He wanders, outcast both of earth and heaven.
> The happiest taste not happiness sincere;
> But find the cordial draught is dash'd with care.[10]

The Greek philosopher Porphyry (ca. 234–305 CE) recounts the fame of a devout worshiper named Clearchus of Methydrium. Clearchus meticulously followed the traditions of appeasing the gods. Every month he offered flowers to Hermes and Hecate and other ancestral deities. Sometimes, he would offer them incense, barley, and grain cakes. Yearly, he would make a public sacrifice. He attended the proper religious festivals. He slaughtered oxen as required.[11] What this tells us is that the people believed there was a specific way the gods expected humans to respect and obey them. Mortal lives depended on the beneficence of the divine. Hallowed rituals of sacrifice, oath swearing, gift giving, and humble respect maintained the gods' goodwill.[12]

There is a Latin expression that is sometimes used to describe this relationship: *pax deorum*, meaning "peace with the gods." Ancient worshipers were generally not looking for nirvana or inner peace. They weren't obsessed with heaven or the afterlife. They believed that the welfare of persons, families, and civilizations depended on the goodwill and favor of Mount Olympus. Humans offered the gods their sacrifices, prayers, respect, and devotion, and the gods graced them with health, safety, and sometimes wealth. This became a circle of benefaction. In some ways, it reminds me of the modern-day mafia. They will "take care of" your neighborhood business, protect it, maybe even grant a loan, but in exchange you must pay them respect, pay taxes, and do as they say, or there are severe consequences (if you know what I mean).

For a good illustration of this relationship, we can turn again to Plautus and his colorful characters. Plautus's tale called *Amphitryon* involves a man named Amphitryon, his slave Sosia, and his wife Alcmena. While Amphitryon and Sosia are away at war, the high god Jupiter disguises himself as Amphitryon to sleep with Alcmena. The god Mercury (a.k.a. Hermes) takes on the appearance of Sosia so he can prevent the real Amphitryon and Sosia from returning home. In the play's prologue, Mercury approaches the audience to give an introduction. Mercury's speech is a bit long and dense, so allow me to paraphrase his opener to the audience, updating the language a bit (but you'll get the idea).

> I know what you [audience members] want from me. I do you favors, I help you find good deals, boost your business, increase your success. I often bring you good news and make life a bit better. I do a lot for you, don't I? So here's something

you can do for me at the beginning of the show: shut up, sit back, and enjoy. Give the show your full attention.

I haven't properly introduced myself. I'm Mercury, sent by my father Jupiter. He asks a favor—which is really a command, because, you know, he's the boss. (And judge and executioner, wink wink.) The favor is . . .[13]

Now you're probably wondering what the favor is, right? Mercury goes on to tell the audience that there can't be any cheating in the game. But what game? Our best guess is that there was some kind of best-actor contest for this kind of play, and "Mercury" was making sure there were no back-alley deals to favor one person ahead of time.

Mercury's character here fairly represents, even if with an extra bit of cheek, popular attitudes toward the roles and demeanors of the high gods in society. There was a pithy Latin phrase that captured well this dynamic: *Do ut des*, meaning "I give so that you may give (in return)." It was all about reciprocity and never deviating from what achieved those mutual benefits. The gods got their due respect and obedience, and humans got whatever they could. Beggars can't be choosers.

Cicero admits that devotees were not looking for friendship with the gods, personal enlightenment, or advice about the path to becoming a better person: "Did anyone ever give thanks to the gods because he was a good man? No, he did so because he is rich, honored, and secure. Jupiter is called 'Best and Greatest' not because he makes men just, moderate, and wise, but because he makes them healthy, secure, wealthy, and prosperous."[14] Sometimes, humans dared to gripe at the gods for bringing ill fortune upon them. Mortals feared the gods, yes, but they also wanted something from them. Everybody wanted something.[15] And when things went badly in life, that was a sign of the gods' displeasure or neglect.

Roman historian Suetonius tells the story of the Roman people's love for General Germanicus (15 BCE–19 CE). By Suetonius's account, Germanicus was a darling of society: dashingly handsome, brave, articulate, kind, inspiring, even humble and magnanimous. When he visited a town, massive throngs surrounded him, men and women, young and old, highborn and common. And when he died (perhaps by poison), there was public mourning and even spite toward the gods. When news spread of his death, mourners threw stones at their temples, smashed altars, and tossed their household cult images into the streets.[16] Sound extreme? Yes, but the point is that the gods were seen to be bound with mortals in a dance of reciprocity and goodwill. Worshipers performed sacrifices, paid homage and respect, and gave gifts. And the gods bestowed blessing and withheld wrath. When that (happy?) equilibrium was disrupted . . . things got smashed.

Overall, Greeks and Romans knew not to get on the bad side of the gods (by doing something like throwing cult statues out the window). We know that the people devoted a cult to appeasing the deity named Febris (Latin for "fever," the god responsible for striking people with severe illness).[17] Some gods were, shall we say, temperamental, and people walked on eggshells around them. One particular concern was making sure to get the deity's name right in prayer. If the worshiper wanted a safety net, then at the end of the naming of the god they could add *sive quo alio nomine te appellari volueris* (". . . or whatever name you wish to be called").[18]

What I have been talking about here is a pervasive understanding of a divine-human social and political arrangement in the Greco-Roman world. Revering the gods was not merely an individual choice but a personal, social, and national obligation. Feelings and internal attitude didn't factor much into that equation. The world belonged to the gods, and humans were guests on *their* property.[19] Everyone had

## "There Goes the Neighborhood!"

The Roman Gaius Petronius Arbiter (known as Petronius) is believed to be the author of a work of satire called the *Satyricon*. At one point in this comedic novel, some party guests are gabbing about how society has gone down the tubes. One person complains that the problem has to do with young people nowadays who don't respect the gods. Because of their negligence, the gods are letting the world slip into chaos.

> What'll come of it if there's no concern for this township of ours from omen or gods? I believe it all comes from the gods, damn my family if I don't. No-one believes in heaven, no-one observes a fast, no-one cares a half-penny for Jupiter. They all shut their eyes and look after number one. That's why the gods have gone lame—we've all forgotten our religion.[a]

This is satire, so we should expect exaggeration and even a bit of irony, but this does offer a small glimpse into popular sentiments about the relationship between the gods and mortals. If humans didn't do their part in respecting the gods, there would be no peace and prosperity.

a. See Petronius, *Satyricon* 44; trans. John Ferguson, *Greek and Roman Religion: A Source Book* (Park Ridge, NJ: Noyes, 1980), 59.

their duty and part to play, from least to greatest. The gods did not *have* to show goodwill to mortals, but they were happy to let the system operate most of the time. Humans were the ones who needed to keep in line, mind their manners, and give the gods their due. Sacrifices, prayers, and offerings were not optional "gifts" but obligations, part of the deal. We find this mentality expressed in ancient Roman literature in another pithy Latinism: *ut tibi ius est* ("according to your right"). That is, do what you are responsible for doing; do your part.

I've tried so far to offer a sweeping sense of how Greeks and Romans understood religion. Alexander the Great conquered the known world and spread what he thought were the glories of Greek thought, politics, art, and religion. When the Romans came along and conquered the same region (and then some), they largely honored the Greek religious myths and traditions, but they "Romanized" them. Thus inhabitants of the Roman Empire were highly influenced by a hybrid Greek-Roman form of state religion. A short summary of the Greek and Roman understanding of religion is in order.

*The gods were everywhere.* Images and artifacts associated with the gods were abundant in Roman society. People had cultic objects and shrines in their homes. Decorations recounting scenes from legends would be found on vases and wall paintings. Small religious shrines were seen in shops and at the market (see fig. 1.3 on p. 20). Prayers were given to the gods at gatherings official and casual. The gods were the subjects of songs, plays, novels, and even graffiti. Philosophers debated the nature of the gods, and physicians and magicians sought help from the gods. Once in a while, a philosopher (usually a wealthy elite with time on their hands) might wax eloquent about how the gods didn't really exist, or if they did, they paid no mind to the boring world of humankind. But regular folk both mocked and found abhorrent such nonsense. Aristophanes (ca. 460–380 BCE), an ancient Greek playwright, produced a number of comedies including *Clouds*, a story about a debt-troubled man named Strepsiades who needs to find a way to get creditors off his back. He decides to enroll in a trendy new philosophical school next door called the Thinkery. He knows these folks are really clever and can convince anyone of just about any nonsense. He meets Socrates, who convinces him that the Olympian gods don't really exist. What Strepsiades *should* focus on is a group called the Clouds, goddesses of rhetoric whom Socrates later refers to as "Chaos"

Figure 1.3. Pompeiian shop with faces of gods

and "Tongue." Strepsiades is taken in by Socrates and tries to convince his son Pheidippides of the value of sophistry. But by the end of the story, he comes to see that atheistic sophistry is empty and leads to ruin. He ends up pleading for Zeus's forgiveness and burning down the Thinkery.

All that to say, you don't mess with the gods. Most people knew that. The gods were everywhere and were involved in everything. The most responsible thing to do was to respect them and go on your way. Do as they ask, and no one gets hurt.

*The gods were divine magistrates ruling over human life.* Romans conceived of the social universe as a big pyramid. On the top were the Olympians, especially Jupiter as "Best and Greatest."[20] Then there were other powerful gods of myth and legend. Below them stood demigods and special human figures like the Roman emperors. Then came the human elites, like men of the senatorial and equestrian classes, and, below them, commoners and freed slaves. Finally, at the bottom were slaves, criminals, and immigrants. Everyone, except Jupiter, answered to someone. You might be lucky enough to have someone beneath you, someone you could boss around. Someone you could force to do your bidding. But everyone knew what it was like to look up the ladder of power and see someone—probably many "someones." You tried to move up as best you could, and you tried to avoid moving down. But one thing was clear: the gods were rulers, and mortals did their bidding, not the other way around. You didn't pray a laundry list of wants to a god; there was no genie in a lamp. You might receive a favor with a lot of good behavior and a dash of good luck. But the big picture was this: the gods were like kings and emperors.[21] You couldn't expect them to have personal feelings of affection or attitudes of grace toward their subjects. They lived to be served, and subjects served. If you gained any benefit under those circumstances, you could count yourself fortunate.

*Humans paid homage to keep the peace and inspire exchange.* Religion, as understood by the Romans, was meant to keep the peace with the gods, the *pax deorum.* Rituals of worship, sacrifice, and prayer demonstrated, on an ongoing basis, humility and reverence, a reinforcement of the cosmological status quo. When you offered a sacrifice, you were saying in essence, "I know that you are divine and I am not."

Those who were lucky enough to get into the good graces of the gods could participate in a circle of benefits.[22] "I give so that you may give." Better yet, "I give because you are a god, but I hope and pray that you will give to me as well." The gods were seen to be self-sufficient. They accepted food sacrifices, but they didn't depend on human meals for sustenance. They encouraged the building of statues, but they had an existence independent of them.

Some of these dynamics are difficult for us moderns to wrap our heads around. In the West, we have the secularization of culture, extreme individualism, and a self-fulfillment mentality to most things. I have found insightful the argument made

21

by modern philosopher Simon May that in the Christendom eras of history, God was seen to be the focus of one's attention and devotion, belief in and reverence toward a higher power. May posits that in the modern secular world "love" has become the ultimate pursuit, and with it the pursuit of satisfaction in life. Finding ultimate fulfillment in romance is a mythical bubble bound to burst; it can never live up to the ideal of divine perfection. Historian of religion Jörg Rüpke, an expert in Roman religion, observes how difficult it is for many of us today to think of religion as a wider socioeconomic phenomenon of political reciprocity and harmony with the gods, a reality that is higher and bigger than the individual. He explains:

> Religion today seems to have become primarily the business of individuals who shape their personal religiosity (some say "spirituality") by selecting from a broad spectrum of religious options, whether these be in the form of religious groups and organizations, or doctrines and practices encountered in mass media (in a book, for instance, or on the Internet). . . . The individual seems simultaneously to have become ever more the thematic focus of religion, not just as the bearer of expectations concerning an individual afterlife, personal "well-being," and "spiritual welfare," but also as the practitioner of special rituals and religious training, and as the subject of spiritual experiences.[23]

In this chapter, I have tried to lay out the basics of how ancient Romans thought about the coexistence of gods and mortals, the *pax deorum*. Rüpke is right: Romans didn't tend to focus on the individual experience of religion, though we will see later that room was made for some preferences. Rome accommodated the gods of immigrants and even new cults. But anyone who wanted to worship an ancestral god or put forward a new religious rite had to respect the Roman way of doing things, and you couldn't do anything to disturb Roman peace. You can see from our discussion of the Roman preoccupation with peace and order that the Romans would have been suspicious of a new religion that deviated from the norm, and there is good reason to believe ancient Christians did just that. This people of Jesus emerged as a whole new way of conceiving of religion and drew a variety of responses: animosity, curiosity, and fascination. Who were these "Christians"? And why did they call themselves "believers"? *Believers in what?* We turn to these crucial questions in the next chapter.

# "Believers"

## The First Christians and the Transformation of Religion

> In thinking of ancient religion we must think primarily not of faith and doctrine, but of ritual and observance, regular festivals, each with its own ceremony, generally, but not invariably, annual, and special observances prescribed for particular purposes.
>
> John Ferguson, *Greek and Roman Religion*

In modern Western culture, we make a natural association between religion and "faith," especially believing in what is intangible, immaterial, and "spiritual." One might look to the Gospel of John for a classic text in the New Testament that might have inspired this notion. Let's take, for example, the post-resurrection exchange between Jesus and Thomas. Jesus appears to all the disciples except Thomas, who is away. The disciples later tell Thomas about what happened, and he refuses to acknowledge their testimony, exclaiming, "Unless I see the mark of the nails in his hands, and put my finger in the mark of the nails and my hand in his side, I will not believe" (John 20:25).

A week later Jesus comes to the same place, and Thomas happens to be there this time. Jesus greets his disciples, "Peace be with you" (John 20:26). Knowing Thomas's concern, Jesus invites him to touch his hands and his side and believe. Whether Thomas does or not is not exactly stated, but Thomas does profess faith when he sees Jesus with his own two eyes: "My Lord and my God!" (20:28). Jesus says to him, "Have you believed because you have seen me? Blessed are those who have not seen and yet have come to believe" (20:29). In 1 Peter we find a similar affirmation where belief in the invisible God is the mark of true faith: "Although you have not seen him, you love him; and even though you do not see him now, you believe in him and rejoice with an indescribable and glorious joy, for you are receiving the outcome of your faith, the salvation of your souls" (1 Pet. 1:8–9). What these texts tell us is that the early Christians emphasized faith in something they could not see and a deep devotion (love!) to a god like no other. For these reasons Christians were going against the grain of the common religious thought, practices, and dynamics of their time. Now, it is true that virtually every inhabitant of the Greco-Roman world held particular beliefs, but they didn't really talk about them *as* beliefs. Rather, your average Julia or Servius thought similarly about how the world worked, where mortals fell on the pecking order, and how they could stay in the good graces of Olympus. They might bicker about religious preferences—but only about smaller details related to favorite powers and which ones would win in a fight. Historian Mary Beard puts it this way:

> Romans could disagree violently, not about whether the gods existed (that was a fact rather than a belief), but about what

they were like, how the different deities related to one another, and about how, when and why they intervened in the lives of humans. It was perfectly possible to wonder, for example, if the gods really did have a human form (or exactly *how* like humans were they?), or whether they were concerned with the lives of mortals at all. How did they reveal themselves to people? Just how capricious, or benevolent, were they? Friends, or always potential enemies?[1]

Romans sometimes argued about the gods—not over personal "beliefs" but over what they thought was true of the gods. But the Christians took their views to a whole other level, "believing" things that seemed absurd, disturbing, and even impossible. This may be one reason that Christians originally referred to themselves as "believers." Today, we take for granted that religion is all about "faith" and "belief." We have "faith" statements, "faith" traditions, and "interfaith" dialogue. But in the ancient world, there wasn't this natural association between religion and faith language. Likewise, the juxtaposition of "faith" and "science" is a modern phenomenon, not one that was taken for granted in the first century.

Do you remember the TV show *Lost*? It was a sci-fi drama set on a beautiful and mysterious island where a group of plane-crash survivors were stranded. *Lost* benefited from a beautiful landscape and seasoned actors, though the plot became overly convoluted and viewers ended up confused, frustrated, and (surprise, surprise) *lost*. Some of my favorite features of the show were the interesting main characters and the development of gripping themes, including spiritual ones. An ongoing theme of *Lost* involved a primordial clash between two main characters, John Locke and Jack Shephard. Locke represented the spiritualist, the man of religion, walking about according to faith and intuition. Shephard was the physician, the scientist, the skeptic, always demanding proof, depending on logic and the laws of nature. Whenever a key decision had to be made by the survivors on the island, round and round these two went. This was a relatively transparent allegory of the modern battle between religion and science, faith and reason, the way of heaven and the laws of earth. This is a familiar dividing line in modern culture and is popular enough to capture attention on primetime TV (ABC, Wednesday nights).

But two thousand years ago, people took for granted religion and religious beliefs (we might as well just call them assumptions). Everyone had gods they worshiped, shrines and images they kept in their homes, temples they visited, and sacrifices they made. All of this was reinforced by law, politics, entertainment, war, business, and family. But in the middle of the first century CE, there was a small group of Jesus followers who called themselves "believers." Before they were known as "Christians," they used other terminology to describe themselves: "brothers and sisters," "saints" (i.e., sacred people), and "believers." We will talk more about these first two terms later ("brothers and sisters" in chap. 8, "saints" in chap. 6), but here we are pressed with the question, If these Christians think they are "believers," what is everyone else?

Obviously, *what* the Christians believed matters, but I think the Christian use of belief and faith language signals a deeper departure from Greco-Roman religion of the time. A number of ancient historians argue that Greco-Roman religion was based not on faith but on scientific method. That is, Greco-Roman religion would have asked for the same things that Thomas wanted from Jesus—sensory and tangible proofs. Clifford Ando, a distinguished professor of Roman classics, explains it this way: "Roman religion was . . . founded upon an empiricist epistemology: cult addressed problems in the real world, and the effectiveness of rituals . . . determined whether they were repeated, modified, or abandoned. Roman religion was in this strict sense an orthopraxy, requiring of its participants savoir-faire rather than savoir-penser;* and know-ing what to do—*scientia colendorum deorum*, the knowledge of giving the gods their due—was grounded upon observation."²

The priests of public Roman religion were not chosen for their piety. They were expected to be experts in performing rituals. In fact, they had to be masters of religious arts so as to maintain the *pax deorum*. It was a bit like being a pro-fessional bomb-disposal expert. It really doesn't matter what you believe about government, law enforcement, or justice as long as you are good at defusing bombs. French historian and archaeologist Robert Turcan refers to Roman ritual worship as "Taylorism"—a form of scientific management. Frederick Winslow Taylor (1856–1915) developed a theory of man-agement that was meant to produce efficient and effective workflow. Taylor offered a kind of mathematical formula to get the most out of human and industrial resources. Turcan argues that this was the mentality of the Romans—efficient and "successful" ritual performance to keep the gods content and happy.³ Roman priests and other cultic personnel had to provide meticulous observance of time-honored rituals.

In *Natural History*, Pliny the Elder comments that four spe-cialists were assigned to provide triple-check accuracy when it came to religious rituals. One person would read the ritual formula out loud, another would perform the ritual, a third would be an observer to ensure perfect execution, and a fourth would be present to enforce silence (*Natural History* 28.11). There were serious punishments in Roman religion for rituals gone wrong or ineffective ones. "Ancient Rome knew about religious procedures or, rather, the processes and formulas required in any given circumstances to ensure the effectiveness of divine assistance. For the Romans, religion was not a belief, a feeling or, *a fortiori*, a mystique: it was purely utilitarian

---

*"Savoir-faire" refers here to expertise in the proper activity and rituals; "savior-penser" refers to proper beliefs and knowledge.

practice. Romans lived in obsessive fear of hazards, the occult powers that threatened or hampered human acts, whether as regards subsistence, the daily toil necessary for survival, or the war that must be waged against neighbours to safeguard present or future harvests."[4] Nicole Belayche sums this up succinctly: "Religious behavior . . . belonged to action and not to contemplation."[5]

Let's look at an example. Romans had many cult rituals for appeasing the gods or obtaining information from the gods. The latter is called "divination," the pursuit of divine knowledge of the future or the unknown. One such technique was called "tripudium." Sacred chickens would be given food, and the diviners would observe their responses. If the chickens ate passionately, this was considered a salutary omen. If they were bored or uninterested, it would spell doom. As legend has it, during the First Punic War, the general Publius Claudius Pulcher wanted to know if his side would prevail over the Carthaginians. He had his sacred chickens brought to him on the deck of his war vessel, and food was set before them (see fig. 2.1). To Pulcher's dismay, the chickens did not touch the food. He knew this was a foreboding sign, and in a fit of rage he threw the chickens overboard to their watery death and proclaimed, "If they don't want to eat . . . let them drink!" (Spoiler alert: Pulcher's side lost to the Carthaginians.) In Roman eyes, Pulcher failed to perform the ritual correctly, or the gods' minds were made up and the Carthaginians were going to prevail no matter what. In either case, belief had nothing to do with it. Faith was not a factor.[6]

There was a pervasive Roman understanding that personal beliefs, best intentions, and heartfelt emotion did not enhance religion. What mattered was what the gods actually called for—sacrifice and compliance.[7] The early Christians had their own practices and rituals, of course. Initiates were immersed in water (baptism). There was a regular ritual meal (the Lord's

**Figure 2.1.** *Publius Claudius Pulcher and the Sacred Chickens* (246 BCE)

Table). But one thing we learn when we read the New Testament is that these Jesus people were absolutely *obsessed* with belief.

> Your *faith* has made you well. (Matt. 9:22)

> If you have *faith* the size of a mustard seed, you will say to this mountain, "Move from here to there," and it will move; and nothing will be impossible for you. (Matt. 17:20)

> Did you receive the Spirit by doing the works of the law or by *believing* what you heard? (Gal. 3:2)

> Night and day we pray most earnestly that we may see you face to face and restore whatever is lacking in your *faith*. (1 Thess. 3:10)

> For since, in the wisdom of God, the world did not know God through wisdom, God decided, through the foolishness of our proclamation, to save those who *believe*. (1 Cor. 1:21)

31

For we walk by *faith*, not by sight. (2 Cor. 5:7)

Your *faith* is proclaimed through the world. (Rom. 1:8)

[The gospel] is the power of God for salvation to everyone who has *faith*, to the Jew first and also to the Greek. For in it the righteousness of God is revealed *through faith for faith*; as it is written, "The one who is righteous will live by *faith*." (Rom. 1:16–17)

How are they to call on one in whom they have not *believed*? And how are they to *believe* in one of whom they have never heard? . . . So *faith* comes from what is heard, and what is heard comes through the word of Christ. (Rom. 10:14, 17)

Now *faith* is the assurance of things hoped for, the conviction of things not seen. (Heb. 11:1)

## Ya Gotta Have Faith

The Christian religion revolved around faith. Of course, it mattered *what* they believed—and we will spend chapters 4–7 looking at their particular beliefs—but it is crucial that we moderns recognize that focusing on belief itself was an extraordinary innovation. But why did these early Christians put such a strong emphasis on faith as religion? Here are three reasons that seem most likely to me.[8]

*First, Jesus called for faith in himself and the gospel.* One clear answer to the question "Why were the first Christians so fixated on faith and belief language?" is that Jesus himself called for faith. In the Gospel of Mark, immediately when Jesus launches his public ministry, he announces that the time has come and that the kingdom of God is at hand. He says, "Repent, and *believe* in the good news" (Mark 1:15). What good news? Jesus preaches that God is going to fulfill the promises he made to Israel to restore their fortunes, reverse the covenantal curses, heal their enmity, and bring wholeness and justice to the world. The very heart of this "gospel" agenda requires Jews to put their faith in Jesus, a gifted prophet, wise teacher, and Israel's own Messiah. According to the four evangelists, Jesus regularly commends people for their faith, and occasionally it is made clear that this faith is specifically *in him* (e.g., Mark 9:42; see also Matt. 18:6; John 11:25; 16:9; 17:20).

*Second, Christian faith was about a covenantal relationship of trust and mutuality.* Another reason why Christians latched on to the language of faith has to do with the language of trust, commitment, and mutuality that is used in the Old Testament. Time and time again, when the early Christian writers talk about the importance of faith, they point to foundational moments in the covenantal life of Israel. "And [Abram] believed the LORD; and the LORD reckoned it to him as righteousness." This quotation of Genesis 15:6 appears in Galatians 3:6, Romans 4:3, and James 2:23. When we look at these quotations of Genesis, it is clear that close, personal faith (i.e., trust) in God was something that mattered to Jews and Christians. Paul especially argues that Abraham was considered righteous before God not because of the acceptable performance of specific cultic rituals (like circumcision or sacrifice) but initially and most importantly on the basis of true commitment, genuine faith and faithfulness.

We can say the same for the occasions where the New Testament quotes from Habakkuk 2:4: "The righteous will live by faith" (my trans.; see Rom. 1:17; Gal. 3:11; Heb. 10:38). "Faith" here, especially in Paul's writings, involves *covenantal* faith, two parties binding themselves together to live in mutual prosperity and benefit. Relationships can and do have expectations, sometimes obligations and vows, but the heart of a healthy relationship is trust. This mentality came to be

---

## Habakkuk 2:4

"The righteous" referred to those who live rightly oriented
toward God and the world.

In the phrase "shall live," living referred to both a person's daily
life and their lifestyle with a view toward eternal life.

The phrase "by faith" referred to daily walking in trust and
commitment to the invisible God known in Jesus Christ, empowered by the Holy Spirit.

---

imprinted as a logo onto the early Christians. "The righteous
shall live by faith *in Jesus Christ*" (my trans.).

An interesting case study in the "logo-ization" of faith language for the early Christians is the way the word "faith" is
used in Galatians 3:23–26: "²³Now before *faith* came, we were
imprisoned and guarded under the law until *faith* would be revealed. ²⁴Therefore the law was our disciplinarian until Christ
came, so that we might be justified by *faith*. ²⁵But now that
*faith* has come, we are no longer subject to a disciplinarian,
²⁶for in Christ Jesus you are all children of God through *faith*."

Paul is talking about a before-and-after phenomenon: the
life of the people of God *before* and *after* the coming of Christ.
But notice here that Paul mentions the coming of Christ only
once (Gal. 3:24), and he focuses more on the coming of faith
(vv. 23, 25). What does he mean by the coming of "faith"? It
can't be personal human faith, because earlier in Galatians
Paul talks about the prototypical faith of the patriarch Abraham. So, "faith" was already a thing in the Old Testament,
before the coming of Jesus. Some have argued that when Paul
talks about the coming of "faith" he means the "faithfulness of
Christ himself." That is, he is referring to the model, example,
and embodiment of true faith that exists in the person of Jesus

Christ. That is possible, but if that were the case, I would expect Paul to have written "before the faith(fulness) *of Christ* came."

It is a bit of a mystery what exactly Paul means by the coming of "faith," but here is my theory. "Faith" (*pistis* in Greek), early in the emergence of Christianity, became a catchall term (like a master symbol or logo) for the unique dynamic of this religion, a relationship of intimacy and mutuality with God experienced through the person of Jesus Christ. This would line up pretty closely with something Paul writes earlier in Galatians: "It is Christ who lives in me. And the life I now live in the flesh I live by *faith* in the Son of God, who loved me and gave himself for me" (2:20). Life with God is lived and experienced through Jesus Christ; Christians co-participated, cooperated, experienced, knew, and related to God by the life of Christ within, and this is what they called "faith." So, Christians adopted the language of being "believers" in part because they so centralized and internalized a relationship with God through Jesus that was oriented around "faith" (trust, union).

*Third, they believed the unbelievable.* Another reason I think the early Christians latched on to the language of belief and faith was because of the emphasis on believing things that were invisible and sometimes intangible, believing things of the future that were not being experienced in the present, and believing things that ran against the grain of society. I call this "believing the unbelievable." Paul teaches the Corinthians to look at the world not through fleshly perception but through the eyes of faith. The world judges the outside, but Christians are empowered to look with deeper insight into the heart. This is articulated in the Old Testament, for example, when the Lord tells Samuel how to identify the next chosen king of Israel. "Do not look on [Eliab's] appearance or on the height of his stature, because I have rejected him; for the LORD does not see as mortals see; they look on the outward appearance, but the LORD looks on the heart" (1 Sam. 16:7). The result is that the Lord rejects the older sons of Jesse and then calls for the youngest, the one who would not normally even be taken into consideration. He is a humble shepherd, but the Lord says, "Rise and anoint him; for this is the one" (16:12).

Paul talks about Christians in a similar fashion. Believers are like ordinary cheap and disposable clay jars, but hidden within is a great treasure (2 Cor. 4:7). Paul's metaphor is like our modern practice of hiding our house key in a fake ordinary rock in the front lawn. Looks can be deceiving. A worthless rock can contain priceless access and power. Or think about the old nickel-and-dime trick. My wife used to trick her little sister when they were kids by saying, "Hey, I'll give you all my *big* nickels in exchange for all your *teeny-tiny* dimes." The dimes are worth more, but the nickels are bigger and thicker. The eyes can sometimes fool the brain, if you don't know better. Christians believed they had come to know better: "because we look not at what can be seen but at what cannot be seen; for what can be seen is temporary, but what cannot be seen is eternal" (4:18).

Paul makes it personal. He admits that once upon a time, before he knew Jesus, he judged and condemned Jesus from a fleshly perspective (2 Cor. 5:16–17). But when he was confronted with the true reality of the lordship of Jesus, his eyes were opened (well, blinded and then opened!). This new understanding of Jesus trained his eyes to see the *whole world* in a new way: "We don't evaluate people by what they have or how they look. . . . Now we look inside, and what we see is that anyone united with the Messiah gets a fresh start, is created new. The old life is gone; a new life emerges!" (5:16–17 Message).

Christian theologians sometimes talk about a concept called *Deus absconditus*, the one God as a God who hides. This reflects those moments in Scripture where it seems like God is absent, does not answer his people, and is silent (e.g., Job 13:24; Ps. 10:1). This phenomenon is climatically expressed in Jesus's Cry of Dereliction from the cross: "My God, my God, why have you forsaken me?" (Mark 15:34), a quote from Psalm 22:1. This is essentially Jesus asking, "Where are you, God?" This statement is both about the invisibility of God and about what appears to be his absence. But the reason for God's hiddenness is not that he wants to be left alone. Rather, he wants to be *pursued* by faith and perseverance. "When you search for me," the Lord says, "you will find me; if you seek me with all your heart, I will let you find me" (Jer. 29:13–14). Jesus also encourages his disciples to ask, search, and knock (Matt. 7:7).

Why? Why doesn't God just lavish his people with what they want, without asking? He wants believers to act on faith and initiative, to pursue the kingdom of God, to invest themselves in the gospel. And they must learn to walk by faith and not by sight. This seems to be one of the key explanations in the Bible for the invisibility of God and the renunciation of idols. Israel must be taught not to fix their eyes on what can be seen but to strain to listen to the living *voice* of God (Deut. 4:12). Part of being a believer, then, is worshiping the invisible God. We have already considered Hebrews 11:1, but now it is helpful to look at the context. The readers are encouraged to trust God, even when they cannot see him. The world itself, the material world, was made by the invisible Word of God. The people of God will often be called to step forward into the unknown, to believe the unbelievable, to do what seems impossible. Enoch pledged his faith and received invisible rewards for seeking God; Noah was warned about events yet unseen and had to trust God (Heb. 11:5, 7). And their worship of the invisible God appeared to be nonsense to outsiders, because often ancient people equated religion with their cult statues and objects, which were forbidden in the Jewish Scriptures.

Ancient Jews and Christians found themselves in an awkward position in the Roman world. They were mocked and ridiculed for not having cult statues, which were extremely common (many would say essential) in ancient religion. This lack of statues may also have been a reason they latched on to the language of being "believers," choosing to believe in invisible things, to see value and life where others saw nothing (1 Cor. 1:28).

## Jews and Christians Are "Godless"

One of the accusations made against Jews and Christians was that they were *atheoi*, "godless."[9] We get the word "atheist" from this Greek term, but that is not the meaning in this situation. It makes more sense to translate *atheoi* as "godless." It is not that Jews and Christians did not worship a god; it is that they were, in the eyes of Romans, venerating meaningless and vapid deities. And the fact that they did not have cult statues meant they were reckless and primitive, a threat to the delicate balance of power in the world, jeopardizing the political ecosystem established with the divine.

The story is told of the Roman general Pompey's conquest of Jerusalem and his desecration of the Jewish temple.[10] There he found "no image, no statue, no symbolic representation of the Deity; the whole presented a naked dome; the sanctuary was unadorned and simple."[11] Pompey was absolutely shocked that these Jews didn't worship a *real* god—because *real* gods had cult statues.

Romans also noticed that Jews did not use cult statues in their synagogues (their regional centers of religious worship). The Alexandrian Jewish writer Philo (ca. 20 BCE–ca. 50 CE) mentions the injustices done to his people under the Roman governor Flaccus. The Alexandrian people came to know that Jewish synagogues in Alexandria did not contain any cult images, and the city could be punished for religious sites *not* honoring Emperor Gaius Caligula (i.e., by failing to put up images of Caligula for veneration). So, an Alexandrian mob pressured Governor Flaccus to impose cult images of Caligula on the synagogues, a proposition that the local Jews passionately opposed.[12]

The bottom line is this: people without cult statues were people without real "gods." They were godless, and a threat to the Roman order. And Jews and Christians were treated as such. Here is theologian Michael Green's comment on the Pompey incident: "The Romans could not get over this. That there should be no image of the god in his inmost shrine seemed to them fantastic, and was one of the reasons why they tended ever afterwards to regard the Jews as atheists. 'Their sanctuary was empty, their mysteries meaningless.'"[13]

## Christ, the Perfect *Eikōn* of God

From the brief comments above, you might get the impression that Jews and Christians rejected any notion of earthly images of the divine. It is true that the Ten Commandments prohibited *graven* images (i.e., crafted religious artifacts like the golden calf). But Jews honored and organized themselves around certain tangible artifacts like the Jewish temple, the kingdom monarchy, and the Torah (scrolls). As for the Jewish temple, it was unlike Roman temples in some key ways. First and foremost, most Jews recognized only one temple, the one in Jerusalem.[14] In Roman religion, temples dedicated to a major deity could be found throughout the empire, and in some ways the idea was "the more the better." Jews, by contrast, believed their one temple in its one place (Jerusalem) signified a special house for the Lord, a place where divine glory could reside. That allowed it to function as a special meeting place between earth and heaven, much like how Romans viewed cult statues as a hotspot for connecting with the divine.

Perhaps one of the reasons Jews were forbidden from making divine images, *eikōn*s, is that humans *themselves* were images of God. The Septuagint* text of Genesis 1 uses *eikōn* (image) to talk about the creation of mortals: "Then God said, 'Let us make humankind in our *image* [*eikōn*], according to our likeness.' ... So God created humankind in his *image* [*eikōn*]; in the *image* [*eikōn*] of God he created them; male and female he created them" (Gen. 1:26–27; cf. Wis. 2:23). The Old Testament doesn't develop this idea explicitly. But it is explored in the New Testament. In 2 Corinthians 4:4 and Colossians 1:15, Christ is referred to as the "*eikōn* of God."

> In their case the god of this world has blinded the minds of the unbelievers, to keep them from seeing the light of the gospel of the glory of Christ, who is the *image* [*eikōn*] of God. (2 Cor. 4:4)

> [Christ] is the *image* [*eikōn*] of the invisible God, the firstborn of all creation. (Col. 1:15)

The Colossians text says of Jesus what one would expect to hear of a cult statue. Roman cult statues were precisely this: an *eikōn* (image) of an invisible (or otherworldly) god. And here are the Christians making this assertion about Jesus Christ—*he* is the one and true visible *eikōn* of God. That doesn't mean that humans in general are *not eikōn*s of God. But it does mean that Christ is the perfect reflection of God, and humans are meant to conform to Christ's perfect *eikōn* to fully reflect divine glory (Rom. 8:29).

A scene in the book of Acts illustrates this nicely (14:8–12). When Paul and Barnabas are in Lystra (modern-day Turkey), they heal a crippled man. When some of the local people see this man fully restored, they proclaim that the two men are

---

*The Septuagint is the name for the Greek translation of the Old Testament that was actively and popularly used by both Jews and Christians in the first century. The Septuagint became a key influence in the writing of Greek New Testament texts.

gods in human form. They think Barnabas is Zeus and Paul is Hermes. Before the townspeople can make a sacrifice to them, Paul and Barnabas shout, "Friends, why are you doing this? We are mortals just like you, and we bring you good news, that you should turn from these worthless things to the living God, who made the heaven and the earth and the sea and all that is in them" (v. 15). The crowd thinks this might be a trick and presses on to worship them. Only after another group intervenes does the mob turn against the apostles. Paul and Barnabas will not accept worship, because there is one God, and the job of *eikōns* is to point away from themselves to the Heavenly One.

## Religion and Belief

Let's get back to the key interest of this chapter—the emphasis the Christians placed on *belief*. Again, it is not that Romans didn't have beliefs. Of course they did.[15] Everyone has beliefs, conceptions of the divine, and disagreements about the afterlife and exactly what goes on in heaven and hell (or on Olympus and in Hades). In the Roman world, people often disagreed about which gods were the most powerful, the most beneficent, or the most clever. Jews were often mocked and scorned by Romans for their unusual beliefs—belief in one God to the exclusion of the traditional Roman deities, and unusual or off-putting ritual practices like circumcision and restrictive (pork-free) food laws. And the Christians were even *more* bizarre: venerating a criminal (Jesus), prescribing Jewish beliefs for Gentiles, and "worshiping" with no statues, no material sacrifices, no official priests, and no temples. But perhaps most unusual of all was the emphasis Christians placed on belief itself. Romans would never leave their fate to chance or to belief. What mattered was respecting the gods, and that was proven through time-honored rituals and traditions. Roman religion was a matter of practice; it was a "hands" religion, not a "heart" religion.

Christians, drawing from the Jewish Scriptures and covenant, believed that *faith in God* was the center, the heart, and the life of true religion. Jesus came as the incarnate Son of God and Messiah to restore the world to harmony with God. When the Pharisees scoffed at Jesus's concern for tax collectors and sinners, Jesus quoted from the Jewish Scriptures: "Go and learn what this means, 'I desire mercy, not sacrifice.' For I have come to call not the righteous but sinners" (Matt. 9:13). That quotation—"I desire mercy, not sacrifice"—is from the Old Testament. In the book of Hosea, the Lord calls Israel to repentance and warns them of divine judgment. Material sacrifices alone are not enough to demonstrate covenantal commitment. It has to come from the inside, from the heart (Hos. 6:6). Similarly, in Isaiah the Lord chastises Israel for making mindless confession with their lips, prayers in words without real personal faith: "Their hearts are far from me, and their worship of me is a human commandment learned by rote" (Isa. 29:13). Clearly, this God does not want mere ritual compliance. He desires faith (Hab. 2:4), hope (Ps. 69:6; Jer. 17:13), and love (Deut. 6:5).

Now, just because Jews emphasized *faith*, that did not mean material sacrifices weren't necessary. When God said, "I desire mercy, not sacrifice," that wasn't a pronouncement ending the sacrificial system. Rather, the point is that sacrifice *by itself* was not pleasing to God; it must be offered out of genuine and true faith and feeling. Fake faith was no faith; and the sacrifice was then just a dead animal, not an offering to God.

We see this emphasis on authentic and true faith picked up and enhanced by the early Christians. Rituals had their value and place, but true religion was ultimately about a deep faith and commitment, all the more so when their religious practices went against the grain of religious practices in the wider culture. The Christians were not just selecting one religion from a menu of options, like a vending machine. By the very nature of their beliefs and allegiance to Jesus, they were rejecting Roman tradition and jeopardizing the welfare of the whole Roman society by disrupting and disturbing the *pax deorum*. This made Christianity a threat and danger, what Romans sometimes called "Superstition," the subject of the next chapter.

# 3

# A Dangerous
# and Strange Religion

## Christianity as a Superstition

The part of virtue displayed in society is called "justice,"
and that manifested towards the gods "religion," towards
parents "piety," or in general "goodness," in matters of trust
"good faith," in moderating punishment "mercy," in be-
nevolence "friendliness."

Cicero, *Concerning Oratorical Partitions* 22.78

[Paul] seems to be a proclaimer of foreign gods.

St. Luke, Acts 17:18

W e began this book with Luke's story of Paul's visit
to Athens, a city full of idols (Acts 17:16–21). Here
we pick up the story again. As Paul is preaching in the agora, the public market, he draws a small crowd
of local philosophers. Some think he is out of his mind, not

worth their time and attention. Others are concerned with what they hear: Is he promoting dangerous foreign gods? Luke tells us that these listeners might have misunderstood Paul's lecture, thinking that he is advocating for two gods, a male deity named Jesus and a female deity called Anastasia (which means "resurrection"; 17:18). They compel Paul to appear before the Areopagus, the "Hill of Ares" (Ares being the god of war), an Athenian council tasked with protecting the city from these kinds of troublemakers.

They invite him to share his religious teachings with them so they can evaluate whether his ideas pose a threat. Paul, of course, is glad to share about Jesus with anyone. With a quick flash of inspiration, he recalls passing by an Athenian altar dedicated to "an unknown god" (Acts 17:23).[1] He offers them knowledge of the unknown. He probably has them interested in his "new" teaching until he starts to criticize the making of cult statues of metal and stone, and then he preaches about divine judgment. The last straw for some of the Areopagites is surely Paul's odd message about the "raising of dead bodies" (17:31). A few people approach Paul with interest (a man named Dionysius and a woman named Damaris), but the majority write him off. On this occasion Paul leaves the city without a scuffle. On many other occasions he is not so lucky. More often he is thrown out or run out of town, or he leaves with a strong feeling that trouble is brewing.

But this is a good time to ask, What's the big deal? Why should Romans care about Paul's strange religious teachings? Wasn't it a polytheistic society? Didn't the Romans believe "the more, the merrier" when it came to adding new gods who could "serve and protect"? Well, yes . . . and no. Yes, the general Roman sentiment was that gods big and small, near and far, could bless Rome and its expansion and well-being.[2] But it wasn't an "anything goes" situation. Foreign cults had to be properly vetted to determine if they were legitimate. The

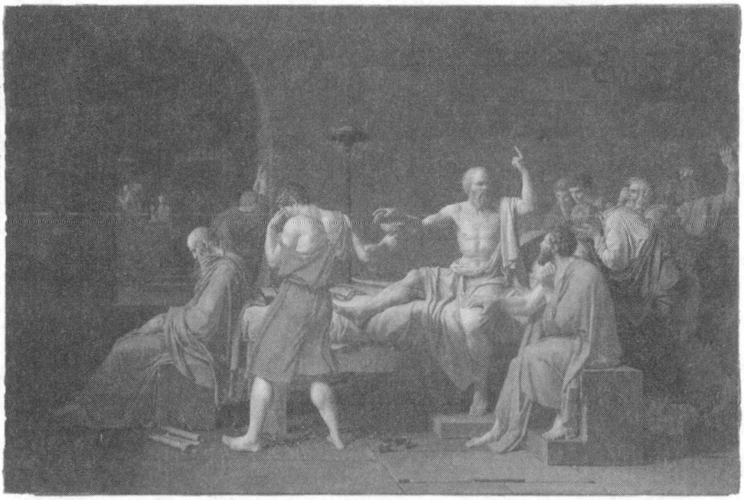

Metropolitan Museum of Art, ID 436105. Catharine Lorillard Wolfe Collection, Wolfe Fund, 1931.

**Figure 3.1.** *The Death of Socrates*, by Jacques-Louis David (1787)

Athenian Areopagus council appears to have played the role of judging foreign cults and religious philosophies that came through this historic city.

About four hundred years earlier, Socrates was put on trial in the very same city, Athens, under the accusation that he corrupted the city's youth with his teaching, was impious toward the protective deities of the city, and taught about new and strange gods.[3] It is true that Socrates did question popular Greek beliefs about the gods. What is less clear is what it meant that he introduced new ones. Greeks (and, later, Romans) were not against incorporating new and foreign gods into their pantheon. What they *wouldn't* tolerate is a new cult that challenged the historical and traditional legends, and that threatened the "pyramid of power" that had Zeus and the other Olympians at the top.

In the Roman world, there was no legal rulebook stating exactly how one should decide whether a dangerous religion was being taught. This is exactly why institutions like the Areopagus council met and discussed these matters; they needed to discern whether a new teaching was a threat to the *pax deorum*, peace with the gods. But we find occasional references to certain strange and foreign religions as *superstitio*.[4] *Religio* referred to proper piety and approved and correct religious practice. *Superstitio* was the label for what was deviant and improper. This was not about adhering to a doctrinal statement but about protecting the Roman people from invasive religious practices that would threaten order and peace. As George Heyman explains, "Roman religion was not concerned with distinguishing *true* from *false* beliefs. It was more correctly understood as an existential category, discerning the proper actions that would ensure the success of the people and the state."[5]

Think about it this way. Today, in America, it is safe to expect most cities to have an official fireworks display on the Fourth of July. Fireworks, as we all know, are very dangerous. But if they are handled by professionals with training, and if certain safety measures are in place to protect the wider population, we can have a good show for all to enjoy. In some states (like Massachusetts), people aren't allowed to handle fireworks on a *private* level. In fact, an official Massachusetts website explains that fireworks are too dangerous to put into the hands of untrained people.[6]

Similarly, Romans believed that the people should follow time-honored religious rituals and that leaving it up to individuals or fringe groups to do their own thing was dangerous. Roman religious piety involved practices and goodwill that maintained the favor of the gods. That must not be challenged or threatened by impious people who introduced subversive practices and innovative religious ideas. Again, there was no legal handbook for how to categorize various foreign practices coming into the Roman Empire, but from the bits and pieces of surviving stories about foreign cults and from the way various ancient writers use the term *superstitio* we can make four comparative generalizations.[7]

| *Religio* (proper devotion to the divinities) | *Superstitio* (dangerous/volatile engagement with the divinities) |
|---|---|
| ancient | innovative |
| ritualized | ecstatic |
| corporate | individualized |
| effective | desperate |

## The Nature of Roman Religion

*Ancient, not innovative.* A foreign cult coming into Roman territory could help prove itself as beneficial to the *pax deorum* if it was ancient and storied, supported by a long history of divine-human cooperation. Remember that one of the accusations against Socrates was that the divinities he was talking about were "new," which was another way of saying they did not have their own ancient legend. Judaism, as I will talk more about in a later chapter, often fell under scrutiny in the eyes of Romans. People like the ancient Jewish writer Josephus (ca. 37–ca. 100 CE) tried to legitimize Judaism in Roman perspective. Josephus explains in his *Jewish Antiquities* that he chose to write an account of the history of his people to show that they have been around for a very long time, have had a durable national government and communal identity, were given thorough instruction in ritual piety from their ordained legislator (Moses), and have since been committed to noble and honorable action toward God and fellow people.[8] Ultimately, Josephus was trying to present his ancestral *religio* as honorable, respectable, and *ancient*.

*Ritualized, not ecstatic.* A second way that Romans judged whether an outside cult was "pious" was by finding out if it

49

had a handbook of rituals and religious rules that maintained a system of respectful conduct in relation to the divine. People were expected to worship the gods at certain times, on certain days, and in certain ways.[9] Seeking "a personal relationship with God," for example, was perceived as dangerous, because it crossed over into overfamiliarity with the gods.[10] We would say they were "playing with fire" (remember the fireworks illustration).

*Corporate and regulated, not individualized. Religio* was not a matter of the heart or inner spirit. It was about each person fitting within the corporate whole. It was deemed dangerous for any individual to make too passionate an effort to commune with the gods. One way to protect the wider community was to maintain a distinction between worship that happened in the household (a preferred family cult) and what happened in public. Romans allowed families the opportunity to respect their ethnic and ancestral rituals at home. But the historian Livy (59 BCE–17 CE) describes a scenario where "exotic" rituals from the East broke beyond the household boundary and challenged or got in the way of the respect owed to the traditional Roman gods. Livy reports that in the year 429 BCE, the wrath of the Roman gods broke out upon the people because of these meddling foreign cults.

> Not only were the bodies attacked by plagues; varied superstition made its way into human spirits too, most frequently from the outside, when people exploited those afflicted by religious madness, by claiming to be seers and introducing new sacrificial customs into the houses, until finally the leading men among the citizens were moved to shame at the generality of the populace. For they saw in every block of houses and in every little sanctuary alien and unknown expiatory sacrifices intended to beseech the gods to show favor. Therefore the aediles were charged to see that only the Roman gods were

worshipped, and this in no way other than that inherited from the fathers. (*History of Rome* 4.30.9–11)[11]

The Roman aediles were city officials who had some responsibility for maintaining order in religious matters, especially as it related to the city's proper respect for the gods. Here they were called on to stamp out the influence of foreign cults, because the Roman gods were angry and hell was breaking loose on the populace.

Another item under this umbrella was the problem of magic—that is, an individual's ability to manipulate, convince, or coerce the divine to wield great power for one's own benefit. Magicians might ply their trade for money, power, or revenge—sometimes all three. For example, in the first century CE a group of magicians promised the people they could stop local earthquakes from ravaging their lands if they were paid a sum of ten talents (more than a year's salary, even for a wealthy person).[12] The sage Apollonius stepped in, divined the problem himself, sent the hucksters away, and charged the people only a nominal fee for his services of curtailing these disasters (how gracious of him). In 81 BCE, the Romans sought to punish purveyors of magical rites with the most severe repercussions. The Cornelian Law of Assassins (and Poisoners) explicitly condemned sorcerers and magicians to death by crucifixion or by being thrown to wild beasts. Any spell books had to be burned and the owners either exiled (if they were noblemen) or executed (if they were commoners).[13]

Keep in mind, when we are talking about magic, this is not coin tricks and vanishing acts. The reason Rome took such a hard line against magic was that it involved an individual's ability to harness unauthorized power beyond human strength—and there were also the financial elements. If the people believed in an extraordinarily gifted person who could control the power of the gods, that person posed a direct threat to the Roman order and to the *pax deorum*.

*Effective, not desperate.* Last, Romans looked for bona fide signs of divine approval, blessings, and prosperity. *Religio* was not about love or friendship with the gods; it was about maintaining a healthy circle of reciprocity. Spending too much time in a temple or at an altar looked like an act of desperation. Piety was best expressed through time-honored ritual, not enthusiasm. Feelings, in fact, were a liability. Feelings cannot be trusted. They are subjective and fleeting. True religion, *religio*, according to the Romans, was about patiently reinforcing the cosmic social order through habit and ritual. These alone produced the intended results of favor and benefit from on high.[14] Anything else was "uncontrolled mysticism."[15] Robert Turcan explains, "In Rome, people had always steered clear of imagination and the surge of emotions in religious matters, fringe prophesying and even theology in general, whether human reason applied to the gods was considered pure or impure. Religious legalism had the advantage of curbing the imagination and keeping dread of the supernatural under control."[16] Notice what Turcan is saying: belief, heartfelt emotion, spontaneous interaction—these were liabilities, unwieldy, volatile, unnecessary, and even *dangerous*. The gods didn't want *devotion*, at least not *that* kind. They wanted compliance and homage rendered in ways that were orderly and ritualized, practical and predictable.[17]

## Judaism as a Strange Religion

We mentioned already that Judaism benefited from having a long history with a chosen people, ancient sacred texts that outline highly regulated rituals, and an ancient god who predates time itself. And yet many Romans looked with disregard, sometimes disgust, on Judaism as a religious cult.[18] Many

Roman writers saw the Jewish people as private, stubborn, and blindly committed to barbarian rituals (like circumcision).[19]

Two issues brought them under suspicion and criticism by Rome. First, they did not have cult statues (as we mentioned already). This was seen as a foolish and dangerous religious practice.[20] The second matter has to do with their exclusive devotion—monolatry. Today we often talk about Judaism as a monotheistic religion, monotheism being belief in one God. But remember, Romans didn't really care about beliefs per se; they cared about paying their gods their due. "Monolatry" refers to the exclusive *worship* of one God alone. Now *that* was a problem for the Romans. While they had a tolerance policy regarding foreign cults they deemed beneficial, it was taken for granted that these religions must integrate into Roman state religion, matching it like a clothing accessory. Or to use a different analogy, it's a bit like adding a track of music to a song. If it makes harmony, great; but if it cannot tune itself to play pleasantly with the melody, then it creates noise and dissonance.

Jews found themselves in an awkward position of monolatry, but some of them sought to demonstrate that they were good, law-abiding Roman inhabitants. The ancient Jewish writer Josephus addresses the matter of Jews not erecting statues honoring the emperor, which is forbidden in Jewish law. Josephus explains that what is *not* forbidden is praying for the kings and emperors and making sacrifices to the one God, asking him to bless them.[21] Josephus elsewhere explains that Jews make sacrifices twice every day for the emperor and pray for the prosperity of the Roman people.[22]

Nevertheless, the slanderous label of *superstitio* was repeatedly used of Jews.[23] They were often viewed as a bad influence on others, with their odd practices (no pork?) and their frequent holy days (weekly no-work Sabbath?). Cicero wrote to his friend Laelius about the dangers the Jews posed to Roman tradition: "The practice of their sacred rites was incompatible with the glory of our empire, the dignity of our name, and the institutions of our ancestors; and now that the Jewish nation has shown by armed rebellion what are its feelings for our rule, it is even more so; how dear it was to the immortal gods has been shown by the fact that it has been conquered, farmed out to the tax-collectors and enslaved."[24]

Plutarch (ca. 46–ca. 119 CE) labeled Judaism a *superstitio* because of the Jews' unusual obsession with religion. The wise worshiper, Plutarch surmises, will pray to Zeus and then also prepare his weapons for war. But in times of warfare, the Jew just sits in his temple like a coward. On their Sabbath the Jews are preoccupied by their *superstitio*, like a fish trapped in a net.[25] Plutarch imagines that Jews approach worship with a somber demeanor, which means they live in constant fear of divine wrath: "He offers sacrifices and feels afraid, he prays with quavering voice, with trembling hands he sprinkles incense."[26] Plutarch pities Jews because they go to worship with dread, as if approaching a hole of deadly snakes or a den of bears. Visiting their god is like entering a haunted house, he reasons. *Could it be*, Plutarch wonders, *that their god could be so overbearing, petty, and easily offended?*[27] Because Jews deviated from Greco-Roman norms, they were mocked as strange and their religion was scorned by many.

## Early Christianity as a Strange Religion

What about the early Christians? As you might suspect (from the title of this book!), they were also treated as a strange and dangerous religion, a *superstitio*: "From a Roman perspective, Christianity was just one more strange mystery cult from the East," Gregory Aldrete confesses.[28] Tacitus recounts the bad reputation that Christians developed in the first century. They committed many abominations, not least venerating a criminal. The authorities rounded up as many Christians as possible in Rome to punish them for their acts of hatred against all humankind. Nero executed Christians by covering them in animal skins and feeding them to wild dogs, nailing them to crosses, or using them as human torches at his night garden parties.[29] Tacitus tells us that their religion carried the label "deadly *superstitio*,"[30] and Pliny says that it was a "depraved and excessive *superstitio*."[31]

You have to remember: Christians had no temples, no priests, and no cult statues. They met quietly and privately in homes. They honored a crucified, small-town Jewish deviant. They had no sacred legends or texts of their own in the first century (the Jewish Scriptures originally belonged to the Jews). They had rituals of kissing ("Greet one another with a holy kiss"; Rom. 16:16) and called each other "brother" and "sister." They went out and intentionally tried to spread their religious practices far and wide. This naturally brought them under suspicion. Now, Christians were like Jews in the sense that they emerged out of Jewish religious concepts and practices. But one of the unique dynamics of early Christianity was that this group of people was not an identifiable ethnic group. Jews had a common heritage, land, and national history. But Christians? John Barclay explains that people like Egyptians, Syrians, and Jews were "mappable," groups to whom religions could be tied; but "Christ-followers, whether Jewish or non-Jewish, are not marked on this map."[32] That made them extra suspicious, a slippery group with no mother, no father, no beginning, and no "where." Suetonius writes that they were "a sect professing a new and mischievous superstition."[33] Barclay argues that in the late first and second centuries CE, Roman writers did not link Jews and Christians together. They were seen as separate cults and more or less separate groups. Probably in the middle of the first century, Jesus followers would have been seen simply as a Jewish group gone rogue, but by the time of the emergence of the term "Christian" (ca. 80–90 CE), we see this group treated as its own entity (and as a threat to the Roman order).

So, if Christians were *personae non gratae* in the Roman world, how did they grow exponentially in a few centuries? Some have suggested that what Romans sometimes found attractive was monotheism or monolatry. This was probably not a strong reason. Christianity defied just about everything Romans knew about religion and the world of the divine. Another possibility is that Romans were attracted to the Christian promise of eternal life. Perhaps, but Christians were not alone in preaching about immortality. This was also an interest of the so-called mystery cults, secretive private religions that promised unique divine illumination and privileged communion with a deity (see chap. 10). Another possibility is the Jewish and Christian blending of religion, philosophy, and morality. Truth be told, traditional Roman religion concentrated on the regulated performance of rituals that honored the gods. It had little to do with whether or not you were a good person. Early Jews and early Christians made reference to a god who cared very much *how* they lived their lives—not only how they treated the divine and how they respected their kings and emperors but how they cared for their neighbors and even the least among them (see chap. 11).[34] Historian of early Christianity Larry Hurtado proposes a bit of a different angle. He suggests that what many found intriguing, unique, and special was the Jewish and Christian emphasis on love. This is definitely *not* something found in Roman religion. Love was beside the point of religion. You don't love your mayor, do you? Your police chief? The loan officer at the bank? No, you respect them. But Christians wanted to say both: God loves you and cares for you, and you ought to honor *and* love him back. That was a very strange teaching indeed. Bizarre. Dangerous— because it naturally took you on the path to *superstitio*. But perhaps this was also attractive and compelling to some. After all, Romans did value love in its appropriate context. When it came to love of family, love was essential and morally good and necessary. Romans did not typically think to connect love to the gods, because, frankly, the gods were all too often cold, distant, authoritarian, and potentially wrathful. So, to consider true and genuine love and compassion as coming from above? That was a thing to ponder.

This chapter introduced the idea that Christians called themselves "believers" because of their passion for the unique and strange things they believed about God, themselves, the past, the future, heaven, earth, and more. But we haven't spent time processing their core beliefs in detail: that is the goal of the next few chapters.

# PART TWO

# What
the First
Christians
Believed

# 4

# Believing
# the Unbelievable

If you confess with your lips that Jesus is Lord and believe
in your heart that God raised him from the dead, you will
be saved.

St. Paul, Romans 10:9

In the next four chapters we will engage with some of the
core beliefs of the first Christians. Now, we need to comment on a few things first to avoid getting the wrong impression about religion and faith. First, religions at this time were
not really in the business of comparing systematic theologies.
Roman people did not have a theology written out in any way,
and they didn't really operate in those terms. Their "creed" was
the activity of pleasing the gods through respect and ritual.
But, at the end of the day, everybody believed something, and
those beliefs affected how they thought about the nature of the
gods, the cosmic economy, the meaning of human life, and

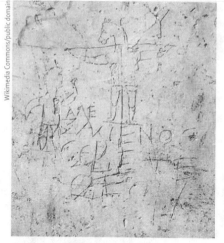

Figure 4.1. Alexamenos graffito (original)

Figure 4.2. Alexamenos graffito (reproduction)

where the world has been and where it is going. Christians weren't the first people to have a theology, but they deviated so far from the norm of wider society that what they believed became a phenomenon in itself.

Take, for example, the famous "Alexamenos" graffito (see figs. 4.1 and 4.2), dating from sometime between the end of the first century and the beginning of the third century CE. It was scratched into the wall of a building on Rome's Palatine Hill. This crude image depicts what appears to be a crucified man with the head of a donkey and, next to him, a worshiper paying homage. The words read, "Alexamenos worships [his] god." The building was some kind of schoolhouse (*paedagogium*), perhaps educating slaves and other laborers serving the imperial household. It has been hypothesized that this graffito was inscribed by a non-Christian slave mocking a Christian slave at the school.[1] Whatever the exact scenario, it is clear enough that *someone* thought that venerating Jesus was like worshiping a donkey—silly and pathetic. In this satirical image, Christian devotion is represented as strange, ludicrous, perhaps even abhorrent. Christians believed things about this man, Jesus, that seemed more than sensational—*unfathomable*. It is true that Christians eventually and inevitably got themselves into trouble with Roman authorities for what they *did* (and didn't do), specifically their rejection of paying practical homage to the Roman gods, but this started with their *beliefs*. And the more deviant the beliefs, the stranger the behavior. So that is where we begin in this chapter. We dare not even try to present a full theology of what early Christians believed. We will concentrate on four essential "strange beliefs" in this and the next three chapters:

The supremacy of Jesus

Cult without smoke and blood

Being possessed by the Spirit of God

Beginning at the end of all things

Right away, many more central beliefs, convictions, or commitments could be identified, including some related to creation, "salvation," and anthropology, but I think these four subjects cover *a lot* of ground and will provide a helpful sketch of how early Christians thought about God, the world, and human life in time and space. And it is specifically in *these* areas, I think, that the first Christians were the *weirdest*.

We begin here with the most prominent and astonishing belief of the early Christians—the supremacy of Jesus. Romans would not have been especially interested or concerned with Christian claims about heaven or hell. They were not bothered even by a claim that a man could be (or become) divine. They had "spiritual" categories that allowed for humans to become special beings through noble deeds and great feats. What they would find disturbing is a claim to *supremacy*, someone or something being above all, master of the universe. And yet, this was indeed the unique claim of the apostles: Jesus was an agent of creation, savior of all people, and judge over all creatures great and small. That idea was a threat to all other notions of power and authority. That idea gave reason to argue—and reason to execute.

## "Many Gods and Many Lords"

In 1 Corinthians, Paul acknowledges that the world he lives in is populated by statues and icons of stone and wood that reflect "many gods and many lords," the great pantheon representing different cultures, values, ranks, and regions (1 Cor. 8:5). One way to get a sense for the extent and nature of these pluralities of divinities is to consult the *Theogony*, Hesiod's eighth-century BCE classic, which is a kind of "teaching hymn" recounting the generations of the Greek gods over time. The first generation includes Chaos, Gaea, Tartarus, Eros, Erebus, and Nyx. Then come divinities like Ether, Hemera, and Uranus, followed by the Greek Titans such as the Cyclopes, Oceanus, and Coeus. After that come the familiar Olympians—Zeus, Hades, and Poseidon—and, later on, Athena and Hephaestus. The *Theogony* reads in some ways like a cosmic genealogy, telling the story of the generations of the gods. But this is more than a simple "family tree." One of the obvious themes of this hymn is the use of violence to obtain cosmic power. Indeed, in some ways, the *Theogony* is about Zeus, his rise to power and ultimate triumph.[2] Hesiod emphasizes Zeus's strength and cunning. Zeus and the Olympians challenge the Titans; when Zeus triumphs, the Titans are banished to Tartarus. Zeus takes Metis as his wife but swallows her whole when she is pregnant, afraid that she or her child might betray him or interfere in his plans.

What we see in Hesiod is Zeus bringing order to the world through competitive power. In the Roman era, we see the continuation and reinforcement of this cosmic ideology. Yes,

Figure 4.3. *The Council of Gods*, by Raphael (1517–18)

there are indeed many gods and many lords in the pantheon of gods, but there is also a pecking order. Plurality becomes chaos without stratification and a clear hierarchy of power.[3] Zeus (Jupiter) is highest in power and serves as leader of the Olympians, and below him are other deities. You can see how there might be jealousy and a spirit of competitiveness. According to the *Theogony*, Prometheus tricked Zeus in order to benefit mortals, and Zeus punished him by hiding fire from the humans. Prometheus stole the fire and gifted it to humanity. For this betrayal Zeus chained up Prometheus to be eternally tortured. Now, Greeks did not judge Zeus as maniacal because of these acts; in fact, Hesiod sings in celebration of Zeus throughout his hymn. Greeks and Romans recognized that achieving harmony and order required conquest and assertion of power. The fittest survived; the strongest dominated.

The Romans had a practice that helps illuminate this competitive sacred economy. When the Romans were about to besiege a foreign city, they would perform a ritual known as *evocatio* ("calling forth"). Here, the Roman leader would stand at a distance from the city and invite the local patron deity to transfer their allegiance from the city to Rome. This would leave the city vulnerable, bereft of the protection of their divine guardians. The plundering of the local temple and removal of the cult statue symbolized the abandonment of their god, who transferred support to the other side.[4] For example, in 396 BCE Roman general Camillus promised the patron god of the Etruscan city of Veii (Juno Regina) riches, power, and security in exchange for betraying his people. Livy recounts the aftermath: "[The Etruscans] had already been abandoned by their own seer and by foreign oracles; unaware too that already some of the gods had been invited to partake of the plunder, while others had been entreated to leave their city and were turning their eyes toward the temples of the enemy from their new homes, and that they themselves were now living the day that was to be their last."[5]

What does all this tell us about Roman religion? It was a kind of "game of thrones," where deities—not unlike mortals—aspired to be on the winning side and would do whatever it took to prevail. It was not a "live and let live" scenario when it came to Roman polytheism. A new (i.e., foreign) god in the Roman world had to prove their worth and compete for a place in the pecking order. Greco-Roman legend-novels are fascinating precisely for their drama and conflict, after all, not their peace.

So where did Jesus fit into this great Roman pantheon? He didn't really fit anywhere. In fact, most would not have a category to put him in at all. Romans had mortal heroes who were elevated to divine status. But this Jesus was not just more powerful than any Jew or any mortal or any hero or demigod. He was venerated by Christians as the most powerful being in all of history and in all the world. This is encapsulated in the ancient confession "Lord Jesus" (*kyrios Iēsous*, Rom. 10:9; 1 Cor. 12:3), or, as more popularly expressed in Christian tradition, "Jesus is Lord."

## Ruler over All

The Greek word *kyrios* is translated as "lord" on most occasions in classic English Bible translations. Over time, the

English word "lord" fell out of use in popular culture, with the abolition of legal slavery and the erosion of the formal class system. Today it is mostly used in religious discourse and in fiction, especially for villains: "Hail, Lord Vader" or "Lord Voldemort." In the Greco-Roman world *kyrios* was a title referring to someone carrying power or authority over another. It could be used as a polite title for someone of high status, similar to the English "sir"(Mark 7:28), or as a title for masters of slaves (13:35). The Roman emperor could go by the title *kyrios* as well (Acts 25:26).[6] And it was used for deities.[7] *Kyrios* reflected power and status, whether individual or communal, less direct or more.

When Christians professed *"Kyrios* Jesus," what exactly were they saying? And what were the wider implications of this confession? We can say that this was more than a religious confession restricted to personal "spiritual" beliefs. Jesus wasn't merely "Lord of my heart." As a communal and public confession, Christians were saying something about the Jewish man Jesus that had repercussions for how they saw the whole world. We can also say that their profession *"Kyrios* Jesus" was not *simply* a statement about Jesus's divinity. Christians did, in fact, associate Jesus with God (more on that below), but titling him *kyrios* said something about his authority in and over the world and was not a binary statement about humanity versus divinity.[8]

It appears that when Christians said "Jesus is *lord,"* there was an unspoken assumption that this meant "lord over all." In Romans, Paul explains that Jesus is "Lord of all" (10:12) and "Lord of both the dead and the living" (14:9). In Acts, Peter recognizes the work of God in the Gentile Cornelius and acknowledges that *everyone* who believes in Jesus can be saved and receive forgiveness, because "he is Lord of all" (10:36). This would have been an *extraordinary* claim in the Roman Empire of the first century CE. Romans did not typically think of gods ruling over *all*.[9] Rather, people commonly thought of the gods as exercising dominion in certain areas or representing certain types of power, though they had turf skirmishes from time to time. But it appears that as the Romans took over more and more territory, and their geographic circles widened in every direction, and as they shifted from being a republic to an empire with an emperor, it started to seem like one person—namely, Caesar—could rule the whole world.[10] Simon Price explains Caesar's ultimate status and expansive prerogatives in this way: "The emperor's overwhelming and intrusive power had to be represented not in terms of a local hero but of a universal god. Standing at the apex of the hierarchy of the Roman empire, the emperor offered the hope of order and stability and was assimilated to the traditional Olympian deities."[11] Now, that doesn't mean that Christians were booing Roman leaders or openly mocking them. But Christian claims were absolute: "This one, Jesus, is lord—master, ruler, sovereign. He is *kyrios* over all, and there is only room for one."

## The Supremacy of Jesus

But what did Jesus's lordship or supremacy really mean for the early Christians? I will explain this in terms of three categories: highest power, creational agency, and cruciform leadership.

*Highest power.* In Paul's letter to the Philippians, he includes a beautiful "Ode to Jesus" (more traditionally known as the Christ hymn; 2:6–11). Jesus, though in the glorious form of God before the incarnation, was called on by the Father to participate in the divine rescue plan. Jesus, the Son of God, would have to relinquish the great comforts and high glory of his heavenly dwelling to walk as a peasant on earth. In fact, the movement from heavenly resplendence to earthly ordinariness would be as absurd or unfortunate as a king becoming a slave—hence Paul's reference to Jesus taking the "form of a slave" (2:7). That in itself would have been enough of a trial and burden, but moreover, this particular divine plan sent the Son to death, even the shameful horrors of the Roman cross.

But that is not the end of the story; rather, it is the *center* of the ode's tale precisely because Jesus's willingness to face suffering, shame, and even death reflects his obedience to the Father and his worthiness of the praise of mortals. So, God highly exalted him and gave him the highest title, "Lord" (*kyrios*). Then, Paul draws out the implications of this exaltation: "so that at the name of Jesus every knee should bend, in heaven and on earth and under the earth, and every tongue should confess that Jesus is Lord, to the glory of God the Father" (Phil. 2:10–11). This ode functions in terms of extremes: (1) the Son began at a very high station; then (2) he lowered himself to be like the lowest of mortals, and even more (3) he was crucified, the most pitiable death imaginable; but (4) he was catapulted into the highest level imaginable such that everyone and everything (except the Father) was *far below him* and will even bow to him in recognition of his supremacy. There is no misunderstanding Paul here: the risen Jesus wields absolute power with no challengers.

*Creational supremacy.* A second way that Jesus is attributed supremacy is as the primary agent of creation; he was there in the beginning, and he helped bring the world into being. According to 1 Corinthians, Jesus Christ is the one "from whom are all things and for whom we exist" (8:6).[12] Somehow, all that exists owes its life—its past, present, and future—to Jesus. This is more thoroughly expressed in the Colossians hymn of exaltation to Christ (1:15–20):

> He is the image of the invisible God, the firstborn of all creation; for in him all things in heaven and on earth were created, things visible and invisible, whether thrones or dominions or rulers or powers—all things have been created through him

and for him. He himself is before all things, and in him all things hold together. He is the head of the body, the church; he is the beginning, the firstborn from the dead, so that he might come to have first place in everything. For in him all the fullness of God was pleased to dwell, and through him God was pleased to reconcile to himself all things, whether on earth or in heaven, by making peace through the blood of his cross.

Here Jesus is revered as the originator of all creation and the center of its being. As a prime agent of creation, Jesus has power, authority, and preeminence over his creatures. What would strike a Roman as incredible (and perhaps insane) is the idea that, essentially, one god is responsible for *all* of creation. Again, if we go back to the Greek *Theogony*, Hesiod sings of the great cosmic history involving dozens of spiritual beings contributing to the formation of the world over time. It takes time and teamwork—Rome wasn't built in a day! But here Christians, following the same line of thinking as Jews, sing of the work of the Son of God, crafting the world and its creatures without challenge, help, or the need for a break.

*Supreme judge.* Around the same time that the early Christians were beginning to write down their beliefs about the supremacy of Jesus, the Roman orator Seneca (ca. 4 BCE–65 CE) penned his essay *On Clemency*, written to the newly crowned emperor Nero (see fig. 4.4). Seneca impresses on him the weight of leadership and the power in his possession—Nero was only sixteen years old when he first sat on the imperial throne. Seneca began with the following reflection on the immense responsibility of imperial rule:

Have I [the emperor] of all mortals found favour with Heaven and been chosen to serve on earth as vicar of the gods? I am the arbiter of life and death for the nations; it rests in my power what each man's lot and state shall be; by my lips Fortune proclaims what gift she would bestow on each human being; for my

70

**Figure 4.4.** *Nero and Seneca,* by Eduardo Barrón (1904). Seneca gives Nero a lesson while the goddess Minerva superintends from behind.

utterance peoples and cities gather reasons for rejoicing; without my favour and grace no part of the wide world can prosper; all those many thousands of swords which my peace restrains will be drawn at my nod; what nations shall be utterly destroyed, which banished, which shall receive the gift of liberty, which have it taken from them, what kings shall become slaves and whose heads shall be crowned with royal honour, what cities shall fall and which shall rise—this is mine to decree.[13]

Apparently, Seneca's lengthy arguments that followed in favor of mercy and compassion did not take hold in Nero's heart. As Roman writers recount, over his career Nero mercilessly put to death his own mother, Agrippina the Younger. His first wife met a gruesome fate as well, and he may have been involved in the death of his second wife on top of that. Nero was known to be paranoid, vindictive, impulsive, and wildly savage.

The Christians respected the possibility that the one God could use government for good and that rulers played a role in maintaining order and dispensing justice (Rom. 13:1–7). But ultimately, believers did not view Nero or any other "lord" as supreme judge; that role was played by Jesus alone. It is interesting that Seneca mentions the emperor as being *vicar*,* the prime agent of the gods on earth who is invested with divine power to promote justice and enforce judgment. Across the New Testament this is claimed solely for Jesus: he was appointed by God to judge the world in righteousness (Acts 17:31; cf. Acts 10:42; John 5:22). Paul refers to the "judgment seat of Christ," where he will pay back each person for the good or evil committed in their lives (2 Cor. 5:10). Caesar, as only a human, can judge based on observation and first- and second-hand testimony. But Jesus Christ is able to penetrate into the inner being of each person, judging "the secret thoughts of all" (Rom. 2:15–16). Jesus stands above all creatures and "gods" and has sole authority to judge them according to justice.

It is worth mentioning here the mystery of the Christian affirmation of the oneness of God alongside the distinction between God (the Father) and the Lord Jesus Christ. Christians have treated these as two "persons," but there is some kind of unique cooperation or "togetherness" about them whereby this unity-in-distinction is a thing wholly different from the "many gods" (1 Cor. 8:5) of Roman religion. Let us briefly return to 1 Corinthians 8 (where we started this chapter). Paul says Christians have the freedom to eat food that has been devoted to an idol, because they ought not to live in fear of so-called gods who don't really have power like the one God. Yes, there might be spiritual beings of various kinds that move about the ether, but in terms of where Christian *religio* is focused, there is but one deserving of devotion. What comes in

---

*The Latin word *vicar* simply means "agent," "representative," or "substitute."

1 Corinthians 8:6 is a Christianization of the classical Jewish prayer-creed, the Shema (Deut. 6:4–9). Jews confess, "Hear, O Israel: The LORD is our God, the LORD alone" (6:4).[14] Paul takes what Jews would consider to be a combination title for YHWH, "LORD God" (*kyrios ho theos*), and splits it apart to see two persons reflected in that ancient prayer: "God" (*theos*) is identified by Paul with God the Father, and the "Lord" (*kyrios*) with Jesus Christ. As N. T. Wright has said, "A small step for the language, a giant leap for the theology."[15]

But how do we explain the inclusion of Jesus in a Jewish prayer about the "oneness" of God? Wright reasons that Jesus "is the one in whom the identity of Israel's God is revealed."[16] I agree, but exactly how is this reflecting worship of one God? And how would Gentile believers have made sense of this? We have already noted Seneca's reference to the emperor's role as one of divine agency. The emperor was a special human chosen to represent the will and judgment of the gods. Perhaps, in some similar way, Jesus is portrayed as God's unique agent, bringing creation into being, maintaining order in the cosmos, and serving as God's primary minister of justice. There is also the image of Father (God) and Son (Jesus) used throughout the New Testament. This also speaks to unity (of family) in diversity (of persons). But in Greco-Roman religious legends, father gods and their divine children are often at war with one another. In the New Testament we find that this special pair is marked by complete harmony of will and action.

## The Paradox of a Crucified Lord

As we have explained before, in the Roman world foreign gods were technically allowed within the Roman pantheon as long as the foreign cult did not present a threat to the Roman *pax deorum*. Certainly, it would have been a problem for this new Jesus cult to claim that their own resurrected leader held absolute power. What would have made it even more offensive and dangerous was the fact that this leader had been crucified. Roman crucifixion was not just a tool of punishment. It was also a social mechanism for shaming behavior that might threaten the Roman order.[17] We have record of crimes that tended to merit crucifixion: slave rebellion, stealing from government resources, sedition, homicide, even unauthorized use of magic.[18] All such activities were attempts to wield some kind of power that posed a threat to Roman power, Roman order, and Roman "peace." For a group of people to venerate someone who was crucified was to glorify something anti-Roman. And in Roman eyes whatever got nailed to a cross did not come back, and it certainly did not deserve the claim of any sort of supremacy.

However, the apostle Paul was not shy about boasting in the cross of Christ as his *glory* rather than his shame. In fact, it became a dividing line for those who belonged to Jesus and those who were doomed to perish: "For the message about the cross is foolishness to those who are perishing, but to us who are being saved it is the power of God" (1 Cor. 1:18). The cross, for Paul, was a gateway to a quiet revolution, a war fought not with metal swords and wooden spears but with gospel power and allegiance to a new kind of *kyrios*. This *Kyrios* Jesus was not in the business of reinforcing a pyramid of power. He preached gentleness and humility, and modeled deference and service, even unto death to save sinners. His message was love that transcended difference. Peace and prosperity for all, not just for the elite or a specific ethnic group or social class. This made Christianity . . . strange. And dangerous to the world order. And also attractive and compelling.

In the next chapter we will continue to explore the beliefs of the early Christians. If a Roman were to visit a gathering of Jesus followers, it would become clear pretty quickly that they had a completely different conception of worship. Worshiping a deity, according to the age-old traditions of ancient religion, required smoke and blood—sacrifices. And yet the people of Jesus didn't really have such practices of their own. This was not an oversight; it had to do with their idea of worship and the way they engaged with the divine. They were not just a new cult peddling a new god to honor. They were a cult *without smoke and blood.*

# Cult without Smoke and Blood

## Strange Worship

> Sacrifice was the closest thing the Roman world had to a creed—a creed in *action*.
>
> Mary Beard, *The Fires of Vesuvius*

W hat does a modern-day evangelical church smell like? (I know that's a weird question, but bear with me.) I imagine that most contemporary churches smell like coffee! But, truth be told, modern Western Christians probably don't associate church and worship with smells. But I assure you, ancient people had strong sensory associations with the practices of *religio*—smoke and blood. That is because material sacrifice was a central act of worship. You couldn't really have worship without it. Today, "worship" in Christian communities is often connected to music. A "worship leader," by and large, is a musician. But the broader meaning of "worship" is about paying homage to the divine, and material offerings and sacrifices were a time-honored way of showing that respect and reverence. We will return to sacrifices in a bit, but let's also note another common form of paying respect to the divine—prostration (kneeling and bowing). Bending down low was a visible sign of humility and service to someone of greater power. We think of bowing in terms of gods and religion, but this kind of activity would have been very common in many social and political contexts, much like bowing in Asian cultures.

## The Business of Worship

Let's do a quick case study to help orient ourselves. You know the biblical story of the "adoration of the Magi." I am sure you remember that they gave gifts, but do you also recall that they fell down before the child? We may have lots of unanswered questions about this short story in Matthew 2:1–12: Did they worship him as a god? Were they revering him as some kind of divine king? And why worship a baby (who won't remember their homage when he is grown)? Did they know he was powerful enough to overthrow Rome? Why did they care about this special Jewish king? (He was not their ethnic king, after all.)

We often assume they were worshiping Jesus as a god, but that was not necessarily the case. Prostration could happen before human authorities as well. We find such a situation in Genesis when the brothers of Joseph go to Egypt to get in Joseph's good graces. They "brought him the present that they had carried into the house, and bowed to the ground before him" (Gen. 43:26). Clearly Joseph isn't YHWH or an angel, so why do they fall to the ground before him?

Worship (homage, prostration) is about power. It is about recognizing and reinforcing a hierarchy in the world. Let's briefly look at the key Greek words that we can translate as "worship."

*Proskyneō*: to revere (most common)

*Latreuō*: to worship (assuming a cultic context, service toward a god)

*Sebomai*: to revere (popular in pagan literature)

*Douleuō*: to submit to, serve a master

As we discussed earlier, what these terms have in common is the sense of recognizing a superior or authority above oneself, just as the magi and Joseph's brothers did. The Roman world was highly stratified, with clear levels of authority and power. The pecking order started at the bottom with slaves and then moved up to elites and senators. Beyond that, there was the emperor, then lower beings of the divine realm, and then the Olympians (with hundreds of other deities at various levels of importance and power). Everyone, it seems, owed homage to somebody—except Jupiter, who often boasted the label "Best and Greatest."

When we look at "worship" from this perspective, it is clearly about more than clapping and singing. According to most cultures throughout history, including Greeks, Romans, and even Jews, worship involves (1) reinforcement of the political structure of the cosmos, (2) appeasement of the divine, and (3) activity fostering a relationship of reciprocity and exchange with the divine powers. Now, this might sound very dull and boring, more like politics and business than religion, but most ancient people didn't participate in *religio* because it was fun or entertaining. It was part of the fabric of life in the world, an obligation that could enhance life, but ultimately mortals were bound to honor the gods whether they wanted to or not. Hesiod once said that you make an offering "so that the gods' hearts and minds might be kindly towards you, and so that you may buy someone else's homestead and he may not buy yours."[1]

When we look at ancient religion from this perspective, we can see it's not about a love relationship with a god; it comes down to business, and the currency is smoke and blood (i.e., animal sacrifice). Ancient worship had a smell. It was thick and pungent. It's easy for many of us today to look back at ancient animal sacrifice with disgust, condemning it as primitive violence. But material sacrifice has a long and distinguished history, not least in the story of Israel. Walter Brueggemann, looking at the nature of worship according to the Old Testament, refers to sacrifice as "the materiality of worship."[2] It was the physical expression of honoring the covenant-making God. This is how a worshiper expressed respect for God in a tangible way. You made an offering according to what God prescribed as acceptable.

Much the same applied for the Greeks and the Romans. Roman historian Mary Beard says, "Sacrifice was the closest thing the Roman world had to a creed—a creed in *action*."[3] The imperial calendar revolved around many holy days and festivals, each one with its expected offerings. You also made sacrifices at parties, at work events, and during war campaigns. You made material offerings at home, honoring the household deities during things like family births, coming-of-age ceremonies, and funerals. The common denominator in all of these cultural celebrations and traditions was sacrifice—fire, smoke, ash, and often blood.

Try to imagine this: At the dedication of the first Jerusalem temple, Solomon offered a sacrifice of 22,000 cattle and 120,000 sheep and goats. Similarly, when the Roman emperor Caligula was crowned (about a thousand years later), there was an offering of 160,000 cows over three months (that's around 2,000 per day). Keep in mind, with the sacrificing of each cow comes ten gallons of blood per cow. What do you do with all that blood? In a satirical statement about Emperor Marcus Aurelius, we read about animals begging for their lives, knowing they might be slaughtered during yet another military parade for Caesar: "We white bulls salute you, Marcus Caesar. Another such victory and we are undone!"[4] Animals were obviously precious in the ancient world, less so for meat (as today) and more for labor. To slaughter animals was indeed a sacrifice. Their lives had great value, and their loss was very costly.

So, why then? Why all the smoke and blood? Why were these frequent sacrifices so necessary for worship? The short answer is, we don't know! The traces of ancient religion that we have don't at all make clear the logic or ideology behind how sacrifice "worked" and why it pleased the divine. But that has not stopped scholars from speculating. Suffice it to say here, conventional academic wisdom points to two reasons for sacrifice as the central cult activity in ancient religion. First, material sacrifice involved gift giving: mortals gave material sacrifices to the gods as a goodwill gesture in hopes that the gods would reciprocate with blessing. As discussed before, the little Roman saying *Do ut des* means "I give so that you may give."[5] (Not unlike the more-familiar Latin saying "*quid pro quo*," meaning "I give this, so you give me that.") It's clear that sacrifice was a gift for the gods offered in hope of return, but *how* the gods received this gift is debated. Sometimes an offering was completely burned up in the fire, and perhaps it was understood that the gods in heaven received it through smoke. But other times suppliants or priests consumed the gifts themselves. In Plautus's tale *The Pot of Gold*, a shrewd slave cleverly exclaims, "I will offer you, goddess Fides [Loyalty], a whole vessel full of honeyed wine as a sacrifice. That is what I will do; but then I will drink it myself."[6] So sacrifice was a token of community and exchange.

Second, it appears that sacrifice initiated a dialogue with the gods. You might say it was the quarter in the spiritual pay

**Figure 5.1.** Hippogriff

phone that initiated a call. That is the theory presented by F. S. Naiden in his book *Smoke Signals for the Gods*. Naiden argues that sacrifice was a form of communication, like smoke signals or Morse code, drawing the attention of the divine. But the sacrifice simply opened the line of interchange; it didn't force the god's hand. The suppliant made a request or inquiry, and the god decided whether or not to respond.[7] Greek and Roman worshipers in cultic settings had to participate in traditions and rituals to show proper respect to the gods, hoping for a positive response, and to avoid at all costs offending them or causing displeasure. Or there was hell to pay.

This reminds me of Rubeus Hagrid's introduction of the hippogriff called Buckbeak in *Harry Potter and the Prisoner of Azkaban*. Hagrid, a temporary instructor for the year, is teaching the Hogwarts students about magical creatures. A brave soul might try to ride the majestic part-eagle, part-horse creature called a hippogriff (see fig. 5.1). But one must treat them with respect to earn that privilege. Hagrid teaches Harry the proper bow and approach to honor the majestic beast. A wrong move, a distasteful gesture could lead to offense, as Hagrid warns: "Easily offended, hippogriffs are. Don't never insult one, 'cause it might be the last thing yeh do." The hippogriff expects and demands respect. Those who comply can ride the majestic beast. Those who don't comply get hurt. (Ask Draco about that one.)

In the Roman Empire, the gods were like hippogriffs. Approach them in a defiant or cavalier manner, and things would get ugly. Approach them properly, and they may be gracious and agreeable. The way the people made this proper approach was by offering the right sacrifices in the right way, thus paying respect to the gods and opening the conversation. Smoke and blood—that is how you managed your relationship with the divine. This method goes back to the beginning of human civilization. It's etched into all the greatest legends and folktales. Everyone did it, no matter the god. It was simply a fact of life.

Except. The. Christians. (*You knew I was going to say that!*)

Yes, Jews broke some of these rules. They refused to use cult statues, and they would not worship the Roman gods. But they practiced material sacrifice daily at their temple, something Romans recognized and admired. And Jews made a deal with the Romans, saying they would ask their one God to bless the Roman Empire.[8] As discussed previously, Josephus explains that while Jewish Scripture strictly forbids worshiping the emperors, it does not prohibit honoring them as great men. Jews found a way, then, to pay respect to Caesar, without compromising their religious traditions.[9] This arrangement appeased the Romans, since it was not a threat to the *pax deorum*.

What about the Christians? They simply did not have the material infrastructure of worship—no temples, no priests, no sacrifices, no blood, no ash, no smoke. Mary Beard says, "To reject sacrifice, as the Christians did, was tantamount to rejecting traditional Roman religion."[10] Now, when Beard says they rejected sacrifice, she is probably imagining the Christian church of the late first century and early second century, when this group emerged as a widespread, recognized religion. We can assume that in the decades just after the death and resurrection of Jesus Christ, his followers, like Peter and Paul, continued with the general practices of the Jerusalem temple, as they were processing their new allegiance to Jesus (see Acts 21:26). And the Jewish temple had sacrifices, of course, in accordance with Jewish covenantal law. When the Jerusalem temple was destroyed by the Romans in 70 CE, public sacrifices ceased for Jews, but many Jewish people then and throughout the following centuries held out hope for the resumption of the sacrifices in accordance with Scripture and tradition. Christians, however, quickly came to see the death of Christ as a sacrifice once for all.[11]

A century after the Jerusalem temple was destroyed, Christians like Justin Martyr were publicly defending their strange and dangerous abstinence from blood and material sacrifice. In his *First Apology*, Justin writes, "This is the only accusation you make against us, that we do not worship the same gods as you, and do not offer to the dead libations and the savour of fat, crowns for the tombs, and sacrifices. And yet you know very well that the same animals are considered by some to be gods, by others to be wild beasts, and by others to be sacrificial victims."[12] Justin also confesses, "We are not atheists, worshipping as we do the Maker of this universe, and declaring, as we have been taught, that He has no need of streams of blood."[13]

The first apostles like Paul had not worked out an anti-sacrifice theology in the way Justin did a few generations later.

But it does appear to be true that the early Christians moved away from the view that the Jerusalem temple was the *axis mundi*, the center of the universe. Rather, with the indwelling of the Spirit, "holiness" could be anywhere and everywhere. Thus, Paul could refer to church bodies and human bodies as temples of the Holy Spirit (1 Cor. 6:19).

When it came to sacrifice, clearly the Christians saw the death of Jesus as the ultimate sacrifice: "[He] was handed over to death for our trespasses" (Rom. 4:25). I don't think we can say Paul had in mind a fully formed atonement theology in his letters, but we do get a clear "once for all" kind of statement in Romans 5:9: "Much more surely then, now that we have been justified by his blood, will we be saved through him from the wrath of God." All those things that sacrifices did in the ancient world—these are no longer necessary because of Jesus. That is part of what Paul was getting at.

I introduced a theory earlier about sacrifice as opening up a channel of communication with the gods, like Morse code or smoke signals. For the Christians, Jesus did this in a perfect and permanent way. If we know anything about the theology of the first Christians, it is that they believed they lived "in Christ" and that somehow, too, Christ was "in them." He was the center of their connectivity with God, so they did not need to seek out sacred space or invest in material sacrifices in order to worship. Sacred space followed them around like the dust cloud around *Peanuts'* Pig-Pen. I admit that's a weird analogy, but try to imagine it. The Christians believed holiness stuck to them like dirt and surrounded them like the air they breathed. They were "holy" ("saints") because of the Spirit of Christ present with them. That didn't mean they were perfect or that they became gods; it simply meant that God was ever near, changing them by his very presence (2 Cor. 3:18).

This was such a strange idea that Paul was at pains to explain this concept to the reveling Corinthians: What he was trying to get across is this: "It really matters, Corinthians brothers, when you have sex with a prostitute. Christ is with you. You are united to the Lord, one with him in spirit. So, what you do with your body matters. You have company at all times!" (see 1 Cor. 6:15).

I don't think it is going too far to say that the early Christians introduced the world to a religious-technology revolution. Before, if a Roman wanted to communicate with a god, they had to *go* somewhere special: a sacred grove, an oracle, an altar, a temple, a statue. Sure, you *could* pray anywhere and everywhere, but you couldn't really be sure that your message was going to get through. It was best to find a spiritual hotspot, as it were. Jewish prayer traditions encouraged daily prayer anywhere and everywhere, but there was still the sense that the temple held the unique and concentrated presence of the Lord. Most Jews tried to visit the temple on key holidays, even if they lived far away. It was *the* place to be: as Judaism scholar Lee Levine puts it, "By the late Second Temple period [including the first-century CE], Jerusalem's Temple had come to symbolize the Jewish *locus sanctus* par excellence. Here was where God dwelled; this was the cosmic center of the universe (*axis mundi*), the navel (*omphalos*) of the world that both nurtured and bound together earth and heaven, as well as past, present, and future."[14] But the Christians had this crazy idea: you could connect anywhere at any time. No one place was geographically required or inherently better. It was as if they had moved from a landline to a mobile phone.

Telephones came into existence in the late nineteenth century and became common household items by the 1930s. For fifty or so years, landline telephones dominated human communication, but you had to find a phone to make a call. This struck me as I was watching the Netflix hit *Stranger Things*, which is set in the early 1980s. The main characters often find themselves in danger, and my natural instinct is to yell at the characters, "Call the police!" But the reality is that back in the 1980s, you couldn't just pull out a cell phone and call for help. There was no option to call out "Siri" or "Hey Google" or "Alexa, call 9-1-1!" In the 1980s communication was localized; physical lines connected devices like pay phones. But within a decade we saw the rapid rise of cell phone technology— instant communication anywhere you are. We take it for granted now, but this would have been mind-blowing to your great-grandparents.

So, how did this "anywhere, anytime" concept of worship work for the Christians? At the risk of pushing the phone imagery too far, we can say that the Spirit plays the role of generating the signal, both the phone's input waves and its output waves, and the signals of the satellites and towers. Christ is the "operator," interceding on their behalf, as Paul explains (Rom. 8:34).

The bottom line is this: the early Christians took engagement with the divine out of the traditional realm of altar and sacrifice. One of the main ways of reimagining this was the Christian use of family language. God is everywhere called Father. Christ is God's Son. Believers relate to one another as brothers and sisters, and they all live in a massive "household of faith" (Gal. 6:10 RSV). So, just as in the home, if you want to talk to the father, you talk to the father. You don't need to make a sacrifice to connect with your father. (That would undoubtedly require a lot of cleaning.) Likewise, Christians could simply connect with their heavenly Father without making a sacrifice. Of course, they needed to show respect, since he was an authority over them. But he also loved them and wanted to embrace them and care for them, like the compassionate father of the prodigal son (Luke 15:11–32). If you have the right relationship (i.e., as a son or daughter), then you are family and you have direct and universal access.

The Christians were not against ritual or place, I should make clear. They had their own rituals. But the Christians had no use for obligatory rituals meant to appease a god or to initiate an exchange. Their rituals reinforced a personal relationship, similar to bonds of family and friendship. (We will talk more about their worship traditions in chaps. 8–9.)

## Early Christian Worship

Let's take a step back from the topic of sacrifice and revisit the meaning of the word "worship." If you were wanting to study the concept of worship in early Christianity, you might go to a library and do a word search for book titles. Much of what you would find on "early Christian worship" would come from the middle of the twentieth century, from scholars like Oscar Cullmann, Ralph Martin, and Paul Bradshaw.[15] That brand of scholarship had a major methodological flaw. It used modern categories of Christian worship and then tried to trace them back to the earliest layers. So the main categories they used for worship were things like sacraments, music/liturgy, and confessions.

But it is better to look at how ancient people understood religion, and then zoom in on how early Christians reflected that context in some ways, but also how they stretched beyond the religious forms and norms of their era. It is true that Christians did have sacraments, liturgy, and confessions, and these three categories are pieces that help fill in the puzzle of early Christianity. But their total understanding of worship far exceeds the sum of these parts. Worship should be seen as an umbrella concept that puts these elements in their place alongside many other things that reflect reverence for God as well, things like loving one's neighbor and forgiving one's enemies. Instead of presenting the worship of the first Christians as a certain set of practices (again, see chaps. 8–9 in this book), I think it is better to talk about three foundational concepts of worship: worship as slavery to God, worship as imitation of God, and worship as participating in God's gospel mission.

*Worship as slavery to God.* First and foremost, the first Christians viewed worship as slavery to God. Slavery, as a human institution, is perverse. We all know that. It is a social evil. But for ancient people, it was so pervasive that it did supply a powerful image for worship. If the prevailing notion among Romans was that worship was gift giving in hopes of exchange, the Christians knew better. God is Creator and mortals are mere creatures, not clients or customers.

Perhaps this Christian language is rooted in the Old Testament, where Israelites viewed and described themselves as servants of God (see 1 Chron. 6:49). I wonder if the apostles found inspiration for this language in the story of Shadrach, Meshach, and Abednego. When commanded to worship the image of Nebuchadnezzar, they held their ground and were thrown into the furnace—and they survived. They saw themselves as servants of only one God, and they "yielded up their bodies rather than serve and worship any god except their own God" (Dan. 3:28). This type of exclusive devotion was indicative of Hebrew religion—"the Lord is One" (Deut. 6:4 NIV). The Hebrew confession, along with the first commandment ("You shall have no other gods before me," Exod. 20:3), is not about belief in the existence of other powers. That's a bit of a complex discussion that we cannot get into here.[16] What is clear is the command for Israel to live out exclusive service and commitment to their one God.

This is affirmed in the teachings of Jesus, who uses slave/master analogies in many of his parables and teachings (e.g., Matt. 10:24). And for Paul, conversion involves turning away from idols to serve (as a slave) the living and true God (1 Thess. 1:9–10; cf. Rom. 12:11).*

Probably the reason the New Testament writers fixate on this conception of worship as slavery is the title they attributed

---

*The Greek verb here, *douleuō*, literally means "the work done by a slave for a master."

to Jesus: *Kyrios*, Lord (see chap. 4). "Lord" is a title of great authority and power, and human *kyrioi* had *douloi*, slaves. Slaves didn't look for benefits or quid pro quo; slaves served at the pleasure of the master. For Christians to call Jesus "Lord" meant they willingly signed up to serve him exclusively and wholly. The idea of Christians as slaves was fueled by that anytime/anywhere conception of the presence of God. If God is with us always—which is a good thing—we are always at his service. Hence, the apostles called themselves slaves of God (Acts 16:17; 1 Pet. 2:16), even slaves of Jesus Christ (Phil. 1:1; James 1:1; 1 Pet. 1:1).

*Worship as imitation of God.* We might be used to or very comfortable with talking about imitating God or becoming like Christ as a normal part of Christian formation (see Eph. 5:1; 1 Thess. 1:6), but in the ancient world this would have seemed like very odd and dangerous thinking. Trying to act like a god was blasphemy. In fact, a key *point* of worship was for mortals to remind themselves that they are not gods but mere mortals. Greeks and Romans did not use the language of "fruitfulness" or "formation" for piety (see chap. 10). Religion was about placating the gods, keeping the peace, and inviting their favor if possible.

But there were some philosophers who scoffed at the moral neutrality of common Roman worship practices. Take, for example, Roman emperor and Stoic philosopher Marcus Aurelius (121–180 CE; see fig. 5.2). In his work called *Communings with Himself*, Aurelius addresses the thoughtless prayers of the people: "This man prays: 'How may I sleep with that woman?' You should pray: 'How may I not desire to sleep with that woman?' Another prays: 'How may I be rid of that man?' You should pray: 'How may I not wish to be rid of him?' Another prays: 'How may I not lose my child?' You should pray: 'How may I not be afraid of losing him?' Turn your prayers round in this way and observe what happens."[17]

It sounds kind of Christian, doesn't it? In any case, as impressive as this passage is, Aurelius seems to have been a rare voice fighting against the popular stream. Roman religion was not about being "formed," molded in the moral likeness of the gods. Roman religion was primarily about benefiting from what the gods could offer while at the same time avoiding any offense against them.

Figure 5.2. Bust of Marcus Aurelius

When it comes to how Romans thought about religion, we can learn a lot from considering how they "divined" the wisdom and will of the gods. Mortals could interact with the gods through an oracle, a medium translating divine revelation. And we happen to have records of the kinds of questions ancient people asked oracles. Marcus Aurelius was right: people weren't asking, "How can I be a better person?" Typically, prayers and supplications aimed at the gods related to travel and safety, relationships and love, work and prosperity, health and illness, and victory in sport and battle (these prayers could be from today!).

One of my favorite requests of an oracle, which was preserved from Greek antiquity, is from a certain man named Agis who asks the deities Zeus and Dione about his blankets and pillows: "Are they stolen . . . or have I lost them?"[18]

So no one was asking, "How can I do right in the world?" Now, Jews did have a moral foundation to their religion, as they were commanded, "I am the LORD your God; sanctify yourselves therefore, and be holy, for I am holy" (Lev. 11:44). But this concept gets more emphasis and direct reference in the New Testament. Paul talks about both imitation of God

91

and imitation of Christ. Part of the energy behind this is the earthly life and ministry of their patron deity, Jesus Christ. The Christians could point to a *person* and say, "I am trying to be like him." Worshiping God, honoring God *took shape* in living like Jesus Christ, imitating him. Imitation is the highest form of respect, right?

Here's an interesting illustration from the Old Testament. Moses is sometimes depicted in art as having horns (see fig. 5.3).[19] Why? Some ancient translations of Exodus 34:29 say that when Moses came down from Mount Sinai, he grew horns. But the Hebrew verb *qaran* could be taken in two ways: to radiate beams of light or to grow horns. It makes more sense that it would be beams of light, since he was just in the presence of the Lord and had to wear a veil when he descended again to be with the people. But one scholar, Greg Beale, argues that this might be a kind of both/and wordplay. While the Israelites were at the bottom of the mountain worshiping a golden calf, with horns, Moses was in the presence of God, absorbing his divine radiance. Moses was becoming like God, shining with divine glory, while the people were becoming primitive like their idol. Thus, Beale says we might imagine Moses coming down the mountain with ironic, horn-shaped rays beaming out of his head, the ultimate anti-idol.[20]

*Worship as participating in the gospel mission.* A third distinctive aspect of Christian worship was participation in the gospel mission. Ancient peoples did not tend to think of themselves as having a religious mission. The goal of their piety was to maintain equilibrium with the gods, to protect peace and invite goodwill. Romans did not really see themselves as driven by any kind of religious progress. The goal was prosperity, and it was achieved through the *pax deorum*.

Contrast that with the Christians, who had this special message and ministry they were called to share with the whole world. Paul uses the language of worship to express his own vo-

Figure 5.3. *Moses*, by Jean Guillaume Moitte (1806)

cation and participation in this gospel mission. Toward the end of his letter to the Romans, he admits that he writes to them with passion and frankness, inspired by his calling "to be a minister of Christ Jesus to the Gentiles in the *priestly* service of the gospel of God, so that the *offering of the Gentiles* may be acceptable, sanctified by the Holy Spirit" (Rom. 15:16). In this letter Paul formally describes himself as an apostle (with respect to the spreading of the gospel to the Gentiles around the world), but here he applies priestly language, as if the Gentile believers are sacrifices made to God, and it is his job to ensure they are pure and holy.

Similarly, Paul talks about the financial and material support for his ministry from the Philippians as "a fragrant offering, a sacrifice acceptable and pleasing to God" (Phil. 4:18).

This God does not want lamb, grain cakes, or wine or vine fruit, something you could buy at the market or temple shop. He wants full participation in his mission to reclaim the whole earth as his. Indeed, earlier in Philippians, Paul talks about the persecution and possible deaths of Jesus followers as worthy sacrifices: Paul's own shed blood would be like a wine offering, poured out onto the priestly service and sacrifice-like lifestyle of the Philippians. Romans 12:1 captures this best: "Present your bodies as a living sacrifice, holy and acceptable to God." F. S. Naidan captures Paul's strange statement well: "[Paul] coined phrases a pagan would find self-contradictory, like 'living sacrifice,' a way to describe how worshippers might imitate the sacrifice of Christ through a life of devotion."[21]

Many Romans would have been deeply troubled by the behavior of these Christians. Failing to give the gods the gift of sacrifices could be perceived as a sign of disrespect. On the other hand, claiming that they themselves were a "living sacrifice" might seem like religious fanaticism. Why mess with the time-honored traditions of animal sacrifice and the pouring out of blood? It is often the case that people don't like change. If it ain't broke, don't fix it. But the early Christians saw themselves as doing what other cults were doing—engaging and communing with the divine—but just better. *Religio*, a proper relationship with the divine, could be about much more than placating potentially hostile gods and securing their material blessings. Paul was inviting Romans and others into rich community with God and with others, the intimacy of a family, friendship-like love, and a mission that could change the world for the better. Where some saw danger, others saw hope.

# Possessed by the Spirit of God

Religions of the Roman Empire were fundamentally expressions of "place"—evolving combinations of rites, myths and legends, and structures located at a particular site in the landscape and articulating the traditional power of that site.

David Frankfurter, "Traditional Cult," in *A Companion to the Roman Empire*

The temples were a symbol of stability and permanence, and of a divine dimension of life. In need, fear, desperation, the individual would be unlikely to turn elsewhere.

John Ferguson, *Greek and Roman Religion*

In the previous chapter, we touched on the fact that *place* was crucially important to an ancient understanding of religion. If you wanted to encounter the presence and power of the divine, if you wanted to communicate with a god and

Figure 6.1. Model of Rome. The largest building in this model of Rome's Capitoline Hill is the Temple of Jupiter Optimus Maximus.

potentially enjoy blessings and benefits, you had to enter the region of a sacred hotspot, a location where legend placed the appearance of a deity on earth.[1] Temples were some of the oldest, most treasured, most well-protected, and best-preserved buildings around because of their religious, historical, cultural, political, and social importance. Life literally revolved around them. Temples were not just locations for sacrifice and prayer. They were often community centers where one might hold a social function. Political events were regularly held at temples. And temples were used as treasuries, storing and protecting a city's wealth and heirlooms under the watchful eye of a patron deity.

The temple represented a terrestrial home of the gods. Cicero referred to the Temple of Jupiter on Rome's Capitoline Hill as the senior god's earthly domicile (see fig. 6.1).[2] As Mary Beard explains, rituals of sacrifice (with all the blood and smoke) didn't happen inside the temple. Those activities happened outside in the fresh air. The building itself was a space that was dedicated to the cult image, the statue of the patron god.[3] We will come back to the cult statues in a minute. First, let's revisit how Jews and Christians thought about sacred space.

## Jews and Christians and Sacred Space

Jews looked to Jerusalem as their special land, where God was especially present in the temple that operated at the center of their religious, political, economic, and cultural life. Jewish historian Josephus explains to Gentile readers that there is a rationality to Jews having but one temple: "There ought to be but one temple for one God; for likeness is the constant foundation of agreement. This temple ought to be common to all men, because he is the common God of all men."[4] For most other peoples of the time, local temples reflected local society and carried marks of that area in terms of culture, decor, and language. But Josephus is making the case that the God of his people (YHWH) is far above all other beings and most worthy of worship—and that having only one temple reflects the essential oneness of this supreme deity. People ought to come from everywhere to worship in this one place, honoring this singular divinity.

Because the early Christians emerged out of a Jewish messianic movement, they had some connection to the Jerusalem temple. But it is important to note that our earliest documents written by Christians—the early letters of Paul (Romans, 1–2 Corinthians, Galatians, Philippians, 1–2 Thessalonians, Philemon)—make no mention of the Jerusalem temple as a place of pilgrimage or worship.[5] When Paul uses the term "temple" (*naos*), he is primarily talking about the church, the community of Jesus, as the temple where God's

Spirit resides (1 Cor. 3:16–17; Eph. 2:21). From this perspective, God's temple can be anywhere, because God's Spirit is not tied to any one location. The Spirit seems to traverse in another dimension, and because believers-in-Jesus can worship in Spirit (Phil. 3:3; cf. John 4:23), worship can happen at any time and in any place. The net effect of all this was that the early Christians, for all intents and purposes, had no permanent sacred spaces. Michael Lipka refers, then, to a kind of "spatial elusiveness" of Christian thought and practice—one of the many reasons Romans would have found Christians bizarre. But Lipka also conjectures that this "portability" of their faith may have facilitated their rapid growth. Their attachment to "nowhere" allowed them to be "everywhere."[6]

## Where Does God Live?

The question of where the gods lived was one that ancient people asked, and they had a number of answers. You might think the right answer is "In heaven." Yes, Romans had a sense that the gods had their own special home far away from earth. But that didn't mean there was no home for them on earth. Just as wealthy people, then and now, have homes in different locations, so the gods deserved, Romans believed, a comfortable domicile in multiple preferred locations. Michael Lipka expresses it precisely right: "Since they were conceptualized as human beings, Roman gods had a place in this world, in which they moved freely."[7]

But the Christians didn't have physical temples, so how did they answer the question of where God lived? They could appeal to the transcendence of God, as we find in Stephen's speech (which got him killed, by the way): "The Most High does not dwell in houses made with human hands" (Acts 7:48). Stephen quoted from Isaiah 66:1 to defend his statement:

Heaven is my throne,
 and the earth is my footstool.
What kind of house will you build for me,
 says the Lord,
 or what is the place of my rest?
Did not my hand make all these things?
 (Acts 7:49–50)

Jews, we know, cherished their temple but had a sense that their God did not formally need a home (2 Sam. 7:6). The early Christians appeared to have a common answer to the question of where God lived: "His Spirit lives inside us." We have already mentioned that when Paul refers to the temple presence of God, he explains it in terms of the indwelling of the Spirit (1 Cor. 6:19). This is reinforced throughout the New Testament and across multiple writers.

All of them were filled with the Holy Spirit and began to speak in other languages, as the Spirit gave them ability. (Acts 2:4)

God has sent the Spirit of his Son into our hearts, crying, "Abba! Father!" (Gal. 4:6)

And by this we know that he abides in us, by the Spirit that he has given us. (1 John 3:24)

By this we know that we abide in him and he in us, because he has given us of his Spirit. (1 John 4:13)

The most extensive passage from the New Testament that considers the indwelling of the Spirit is Romans 8:9–11: "But you are not in the flesh; you are in the Spirit, since the Spirit of God dwells in you. Anyone who does not have the Spirit of Christ does not belong to him. But if Christ is in you, though the body is dead because of sin, the Spirit is life because of

99

righteousness. If the Spirit of him who raised Jesus from the dead dwells in you, he who raised Christ from the dead will give life to your mortal bodies also through his Spirit that dwells in you."

Where did this notion of Spirit indwelling come from? There are clear echoes of imagery used in Ezekiel 36:25–28, where the Lord promises to Israel that he will purify his people and give them new life.

> I will sprinkle clean water upon you, and you shall be clean from all your uncleannesses, and from all your idols I will cleanse you. A new heart I will give you, and a new spirit I will put within you; and I will remove from your body the heart of stone and give you a heart of flesh. I will put my spirit within you, and make you follow my statutes and be careful to observe my ordinances. Then you shall live in the land that I gave to your ancestors; and you shall be my people, and I will be your God.

The idea of having a divine spirit reside within a vessel was very common in the ancient world.[8] Before we go deeper into what it meant for Christians to claim the indwelling of the Spirit, it is crucial that we understand how Romans thought about the presence of the gods in their cult statues.

## Divine Made Stone

Before there was the Christian notion of "Word made flesh," ancient people conceived of the earthly presence of their gods through statues—you might say "divine made stone." An artisan was hired to shape a rock or a piece of wood or metal into the form of a god. People seemed to know human fabrication was involved, but many believed that somehow this object became a god's vessel on earth—their avatar, if you will.[9] Understanding how statues were used and thought of more generally at the time is important in grasping how statues functioned as divine avatars.[10] The Roman conception drew from the Greek tradition that came before it, so that is a good place to begin.

Greeks viewed statues as more than just objects made by human hands. While it would have been clear that any stone or wooden statue had a human creator, there was the possibility it could become imbued with the spirit or persona of a real person. For example, Greek travel writer Pausanias recounts the story of a famous Greek athlete named Theagenes. After this hero died, his family had a bronze statue made to honor his life. Theagenes had a particular enemy who wanted to get back at him and did so by beating the statue. According to Pausanias, the statue fought back and killed the man. (Wait, it gets weirder.) The children of the murdered man took the statue to court. The court found it guilty and mandated a punishment of exile.[11] Who knows what parts of this story are true, but it does reveal a Greek conception of statues as social agents that allowed a person to be present when they were not there in the flesh.[12] It was not unusual for Greeks to bury a statue in a grave as a substitute for a corpse when a body could not be recovered (as with a drowning at sea).[13] Statues in these situations were not just symbolic objects, poor substitutes; Greeks would have understood and treated them as vessels or conduits of the living being of the person.

When it comes to interaction with the gods, Nigel Spivey offers a fascinating case study involving vase art from the city of Apulia in Italy. A fourth-century BCE vase was discovered with a picture of the temple of Apollo (see fig. 6.2 on p. 102). There are two images of Apollo, the sun god, one inside the temple and one outside. The image inside is a depiction of what the Apollo statue in the real temple looked like, and the image outside is probably portraying the god who lives on Mount Olympus. But Spivey argues that the point of this art is

**Figure 6.2.** Amphora (vase) of cult statue in a temple. Both of the figures depict Apollo. Spivey considers the possibility that the figure in the temple is the cult statue and the one outside is the living god Apollo.

not to identify the real god (outside the temple) but, rather, to recognize that both of them are the one Apollo; hence, Spivey refers to the temple Apollo as a "bionic" statue, allowing the life of the god to be really present with the worshiper.[14]

This Greco-Roman notion of living divine statues helps explain numerous legends and stories of cult statues acting like they were possessed by living beings. One account testifies to a statue of Athena that closed its eyes.[15] It is said that the statue of the goddess Fortuna spoke in perfect Latin to her female supplicants, affirming their commitment.[16] Roman historian Dio Cassius (ca. 165–ca. 235 CE) recorded a witness who saw the statue of Minerva bleed.[17] With these kinds of stories in Roman memory, it is no wonder that people would treat their cult statues *as* the gods themselves, clothing them with fine attire and taking them to the bathroom or outside the temple for some fresh air. Reportedly, it was the custom in the Capitoline temple for a steward to update the statue of Jupiter on the time of day and the names of important people entering the building.[18] One of my favorite stories along these lines happened in the fourth-century BCE siege of Tyre, in Phoenicia. As Alexander the Great was on the brink of conquering the city, the local Tyrians were so worried that their patron god

## Saith the Statue of Vertumnus

Romans worshiped Vertumnus as a god of seasons, gardens, and fertility (see fig. 6.3). The Latin poet Sextus Propertius (ca. 50–15 BCE) imagines what it would have been like for the god Vertumnus to speak from the body of a statue. He offers an extended first-person monologue from the mouth of the statue.[a] Vertumnus acknowledges that he can take many forms, including this form. He comments on the pleasant view from where the statue is placed (a great view of the Roman forum!). He mentions that the various statues he has inhabited have different features, clothing, and accessories, and he appreciates the variety. Sometimes these earthly bodies are wood, sometimes bronze.

Yair-haklai/Wikimedia Commons/CC by SA 3.0

Propertius offers a fascinating glimpse into how Romans thought about the unique nature of these statues. It is clear that they knew the statue was not going to walk away or pick up a weapon. A worshiper could come back day after day and assume the statue would be there. At the same time, they clearly saw these statues as more than monuments. The deity could, in some real sense, take up residence in the statue and see the world through the statue's eyes, if you will.[b]

Figure 6.3. *Vertumnus* by Francesco Penso (1717)

a. See Propertius, *The Elegies* 4.2.
b. For an extended discussion of Roman views on cult image, ontology, and agency, see Jörg Rüpke, *On Roman Religion: Lived Religion and the Individual in Ancient Rome* (New York: Cornell University Press, 2016), 45–51.

Apollo would abandon them in their greatest hour of need that they chained their statue of Apollo to the ground with heavy bonds so that he could not fly away.[19]

What does all this have to do with a Christian understanding of the presence of God? Greeks and Romans would have been able to understand the Christian claim that the Spirit, the animating presence of God, actually lives in bodies—not statues but the flesh bodies of believers. Christians could point to pagan cult statues, to idols, and say, "You see those statues? *We* are like that. God lives in *us*." Does that sound crazy and weird? This concept is probably present at the very beginning of the Bible, Genesis 1. When it is said that humans are made in the "image of God," an ancient reader would make a natural association with statues as images of a person.[20]

Christians claimed that it was specifically the Spirit of *Christ* that lived within them (Rom. 8:9). No single human, limited by nature and corrupted by sin, could possess the Spirit in all its fullness; only the unique God-man, Christ, could claim that privilege. As Colossians expresses, "[Christ] is the image of the invisible God" (Col. 1:15). That idea resembles quite closely how Roman people would have understood the avatar-like being and function of a cult statue. It was the visible and tangible being of an otherworldly god. Jesus was the perfect incarnation of the great invisible God. But as Jesus ascended after his resurrection, he is present again in his people who are "the body of Christ"—not physically (Jesus still has a body in heaven) but by extension as the Spirit lives and works within this people.

Christians, as vessels of the Holy Spirit, are not perfect but are made more and more whole and complete through the transformative power of God's Spirit, thus becoming more and more like Christ, who is the perfect image of God (2 Cor. 3:18).

So, when people ask, "Where is your god?" Christians have multiple answers at once. He is in heaven, the special dwelling place of God. But God is also spirit, so he can be anywhere in the cosmos that he likes. And he lives within his people. Christians are walking temples, holy vessels of his presence through the Spirit that he gave to his people. The biggest temple one could imagine, let alone frail human bodies, cannot fully contain God's massive being. And yet by his grace he has deposited his living Spirit in mortal bodies. It is for this reason that Christians called one another "saints" (*hagioi*)—not because they believed themselves to be saintly in the sense of spiritual perfection but as a reminder of the privilege of having God live within them, a home of bone and flesh and blood.

There is a special privilege in being an embodied temple of God's Spirit but also a responsibility. This body and life must be kept holy. Paul warns the Corinthians (more than once!) that they must live holy and pure lives because of God's presence in them. To paraphrase 2 Corinthians 6:14–16, Paul is saying, "Can justice and injustice cooperate? Can light and darkness intersect? Can Christ be paired with Satan? Can the temple of God (our bodies) form a bond with idols?" The clear answer is "Never!" For God to be welcome and present, the host (Christians) must be pure and holy (7:1). For this reason, God placed a strict calling on Christians to maintain sexual purity: "For God did not call us to impurity but in holiness" (1 Thess. 4:7). This is one of several reasons why Christians emphasized a holy lifestyle. If God is always near, Christian behavior must honor that presence (1 Cor. 6:15).

## God's Empowering and Gracious Spirit

All along I have presented *religio* as the human concern with honoring and revering the gods and as the maintaining of peace between the divine and mortal realms. Rituals of sacrifice and prayers of devotion supported these purposes, but this was not the only reason humans were interested in the divine. There was also the possibility of obtaining, wielding, and controlling the power of a divine spirit. The academic language for this is "magic." It refers not to party tricks for entertainment and personal thrill, as we typically use the word today, but to the channeling of numinous energy toward self-gain. Magic of this kind was of widespread interest in the Roman world. How do we know? We have lots of evidence of the use (and government regulation) of spells, charms, incantations, amulets, and wands. We could talk about many examples of this, but to start off I will mention the dangers of the "evil eye."

There was the belief in popular Greco-Roman culture that if you looked at someone with great focus and intensity, you could curse them with your gaze, the "evil eye" (see fig. 6.4). Plutarch, for example, recounts how certain nefarious men like to harm children with the evil eye, children being particularly susceptible due to their small size. As for the effects, "Those on the receiving end of a look, a breath, or an utterance from them wasted away and fell sick."[21] Plutarch goes on to explain that the power of the evil eye emitted a "blighting ray," usually motivated by envy. It had such mercurial potency that sometimes it could "fire" inadvertently, harming or even killing a loved one by accident. The evil eye was also known to bewitch or hypnotize.[22] How could you protect yourself? Some say by spitting; others say by wearing special amulets, or the skin of a hyena.[23] The apostle Paul actually borrows language from this phenomenon when he chastises the Galatians: "You foolish Galatians! Who has cast an evil spell on you?" (3:1, my trans.). Paul probably doesn't mean this literally; he was writing a letter to them because he thought they could be reasoned with. But he used familiar "hexing" language to address the seriousness of their dangerous and hasty deviation from the true gospel. He was saying, "Snap out of the 'spell' those outsiders cast on you!"

Figure 6.4. In this ancient fresco, we find a man going to the bathroom and a deity offering protection. The inscription reads, "Cacator cave malu(m)" (Anyone crapping, beware of evil). This is probably a warning to people to relieve themselves in the correct place, in private; otherwise, someone watching might cast the evil eye on them.

As we look at other parts of the New Testament, we find more references to magic in the Roman world; two incidents in the book of Acts are instructive.

## Simon the Magician (Acts 8:9–24)

A certain Simon of Samaria was known as a magician and aspired to great power. He encountered the apostles, heard the good news, and was baptized. He took special interest in the miracles performed by Philip. After John and Peter were sent to Samaria to assist in preaching and caring for new believers, Simon took notice of the giving of the Spirit at the hands of the apostles. Simon, an experienced magician, saw this as an opportunity to take his abilities to the next level, so he of-fered to pay the apostles in exchange for the secrets to their powers. Peter rebuked Simon: "You can't buy God's gracious gift!" Peter saw wickedness in Simon's heart and warned him to repent before God.

## The Girl with the Python Spirit (Acts 16:16–18)

The second episode takes place in Philippi, where Paul and Silas are preaching the gospel. They encounter a slave girl who has a *pneuma pythōna*, a spirit of divination, literally a "python spirit." This is language that traces back to the famous Oracle of Delphi, where legend says that the god Apollo killed the great python protector of the sacred place.

This Philippian girl can tell the future for the right price (paid to her owners). When she encounters the apostles, the spirit possessing her forces her to shout, "These men are slaves of the Most High God, who proclaim to you a way of salvation" (Acts 16:17). Though this spirit is apparently very powerful, Paul casts it out handily in the name of Jesus. This upsets the girl's owners, who lost this lucrative spirit, so they take action and complain to the city leaders about these troublemaking outsiders. Paul and Silas are beaten and imprisoned.

What I find fascinating about this story is the intersection of things like magic, economics, and politics. This reminds me of the incident a few chapters later in Acts where a group of magicians come to faith in Jesus and demonstrate their commitment by burning their spell books: "When the value of these books was calculated, it was found to come to fifty thousand silver coins" (19:19). In modern terms, that would be equivalent to five to ten million dollars. Put simply, magic was big money because magic offered power.

## How the Holy Spirit Works

As we think about the Christian understanding of the indwelling of the Holy Spirit, it is easy to see a remarkable contrast between the Christian conception of the Spirit and the Roman idea of the gods.

*The Holy Spirit gives freely and to all equally.* In a competitive world, where people are tempted to hoard power for themselves and steal it from others, one can see how wielding the might of the gods could become a temptation. Magicians were not moonlighting for fun and "hobby income." This was a serious business. In fact, magicians were among those whom Roman leaders classified as worthy of crucifixion, one of the most elaborate forms of execution. Why? Because they could wield almost limitless power in an unregulated manner. Extraordinary power in the hands of just a few could wreak havoc on the social order and even the *pax deorum*.

We can make a clear contrast with that famous scene of Pentecost in the book of Acts, where the mighty Spirit of God rests on *all* who were there in that upper room, each and every one, great or small, rich or poor, male or female (2:1–13, esp. 2:3). "All of them were filled with the Holy Spirit and began to speak in other languages, as the Spirit gave them ability" (2:4). No money changed hands. There were no tiers of empowerment; the most power did not go to the wealthiest or the highest in status. There is an equality dynamic present in this inaugural event for the church. The first thing the church comes to learn about the empowering Spirit is that each person receives the Spirit freely and is empowered equally.

*The Holy Spirit gives for the good.* Another clear distinctive of the Holy Spirit's work is that it is all *for the good*. While most people at the time believed that the cosmos was populated by all manner of spirits, powers, ghosts, and phantasms, good and evil, vying for power, Christians believed that this one great

Spirit of spirits is gracious and gives only to bless and build up. The Holy Spirit cannot be manipulated or channeled to harm.[24]

Paul lays out nicely the benevolent work of the Spirit. As he explains to the Corinthians (1 Cor. 12:4–11), the one Spirit gives specially tailored gifts to each person. Each person is graced with something to offer the community, and the sum of it all is blessing for the common good. This is where Paul's famous body metaphor comes into play (12:12–31). There is *one* Spirit to help make different people learn to cooperate as one communal body. Some "members" are like an eye or a foot or a heart; some are more prominent in role and visibility, others less so, but the whole cannot operate unless all parts are there. And the Spirit is responsible for bringing all these parts into meaningful cooperation so that the larger body can live well.

*The Holy Spirit empowers through relationship.* Christians believed that the Spirit was not a force to be controlled by worshipers but, rather, a *person* who empowered and influenced in relationship. The Holy Spirit was given to believers as an ever-present guide and coach and as a personal testimony to God's love (Rom. 5:5; 15:30). The Spirit often played the role of a host who supported and fostered a vibrant and rich community of peace, love, mutuality, justice, and goodness (14:17).

While Christians did not pray directly to the Spirit, they recognized the indwelling of God's Spirit, who empowered, formed, and shaped their lives and who served as an internal "hotspot" for communing with God. If Romans were anxious about peace with the gods, Christians believed themselves to already be at peace with God through the gospel of Jesus Christ, and the presence of the Spirit was God's eternal sign of that peace.

# Beginning at the End of All Things

*A Strange Reckoning of Time*

> This is the end—for me, the beginning of life.
>
> Dietrich Bonhoeffer, *The Collected Sermons*
> *of Dietrich Bonhoeffer**

There is an old myth that still gets passed around, and it is worth debunking. It goes something like this: ancient peoples and religions organized their calendars and conceptions of time according to nature and the agricultural seasonal cycles, and then Judaism and Christianity came along and focused on timeline events like creation, the exodus, and the cross. This myth is kind of true and kind of false. Put another way, we will eventually argue that Jews and Christians did indeed have a fresh take on time, but the cyclical-versus-linear

---

*These were the last recorded words of German theologian Dietrich Bonhoeffer.

Figure 7.1. The Shanghai copy of the sculpture *Nobility of Time*, by Salvador Dalí (1977)

dichotomy is just plain wrong. The reality is that all peoples in all times have had a sense for both the cyclical and the linear/progressive aspects of time. Even today we chart days and months on a cycle, but years in a line. For centuries, people have wrestled with the mystery of time, which can move slowly sometimes and quickly other times, and yet it is understood that the hands of the clock or the movement of the sun doesn't actually change speed.\* Time is the great constant. Everyone knows it, experiences it, lives and dies by it.

You may be familiar with the twentieth-century artist Salvador Dalí's obsession with clocks and watches and his trademark depiction of melting clocks (see fig. 7.1).

\*Of course, we know today that the earth moves, not the sun; but ancient people would have thought of time progressing in sync with the movement of the sun.

Dalí never fully revealed the intent of this imagery in his art, but the best explanation I have heard is that it represents both the constancy and the flexibility of time. (Rumor has it that the inspiration for these floppy timepieces involves Dalí's observation of cheese melting in the sun.)

Another way to think about the dynamic nature of time is to consider the power involved in *who* decides the calendar and clock system, *what* it is based on, and *what* events and occasions ought to be remembered and celebrated. Consider the matter today, in the twenty-first century. If a new movie comes out on a streaming platform on a particular day, which time zone marks the exact release hour? Should the release focus on London? New York? Los Angeles? Hong Kong?

During the early years of Rome, and into the era of the republic (509–27 BCE), virtually all the national holidays were concentrated on honoring various gods (see the discussion and table later in the chapter), but in the imperial age, especially the first century CE, the emperors gravitated toward instituting public celebrations of their own war victories and accomplishments. Time became fixated on Roman power, the might of the people and their leadership. The "clock" not only pointed to a day or an hour but turned attention to the emperor as the ruler of space *and* time.

In a sense the early Christians had a similar mentality. Time *should* mark what one values the most, the ruler of the world. But in their minds this ruler did not sit on a throne in an imperial Roman palace. He ruled from much higher above and promised to come to be with his people soon to change all things, including time. But that's getting ahead of ourselves. Let's go back to Roman religion and Roman timekeeping.

## Time Dedicated to the *Pax Deorum*

"A life without festivals is like a road without inns." (Democritus)[1]

"Each [calendrical] festival, with all its different associations, presented and represented a picture of Romanness—linking the past with the present, and bringing together apparently diverse aspects of the Roman religious and cultural tradition. In a sense, the ritual calendar as a whole can be seen as a conceptual pageant of Rome and what it was to be Roman." (Mary Beard)[2]

Romans basically invented the annual calendar that we use today, with the year broken down into months and days that add up to about 360. In the modern world our orientation toward the months of the year is related to seasons, work and school routines, and holidays. But in the Roman world, time primarily revolved around the gods, as with all things. Even many of the names of the months come from "above." January is named after Janus, the god of transitions (see fig. 7.2). February honors the goddess Februa, a deity of purification. March is Mars, June is Juno, and so on. Time belonged to the powers, and mortal life was scheduled to recognize the gods who sustained and protected food, shelter, business, statehood, and family.[3] It's no wonder, then, that Romans had numerous official holidays, where inhabitants took time away from work to attend festivals of sacrifice, purification, feasting, merriment, and prayer.

A full list of Roman holy days shows how serious the Romans were about these observances. On

Figure 7.2. The two-faced portrait of the Roman god Janus depicted on a second-century BCE coin
CNG Classical Numismatic Group/Wikimedia Commons/CC by 2.5

114

average, Romans observed about four festivals a month. This is ironic because they often accused Jews of being lazy for taking a day off per week for their Sabbath observance while they themselves took off almost the same number of days per year.

A few of these festivals were commemorations of historical events, such as Parilia, remembering the founding of Rome

| Month | Festival | Month | Festival |
|---|---|---|---|
| January | Agonalia (Janus) | June | Vestalia |
| | Carmentalia (2×) | | Matralia |
| February | Parentalia | July | Poplifugia |
| | Lupercalia | | Lucaria |
| | Quirinalia | | Neptunalia |
| | Feralia | | Furrinalia |
| | Terminalia | August | Portunalia |
| | Regifugium | | Vinalia |
| | Equirria | | Consualia |
| March | Equirria | | Volcanalia |
| | Anna Perenna | | Lightness to Darkness |
| | Liberalia | | Opiconsivia |
| | Agonalia (Mars) | | Volturnalia |
| | Quinquatrus | October | Meditrinalia |
| | Tubilustrium | | Fontinalia |
| April | Megalesia | | Armilustrium |
| | Fordicidia | December | Agonalia (Sol) |
| | Cerialia | | Consualia |
| | Parilia | | Saturnalia |
| | Vinalia | | Opalia |
| | Robigalia | | Divalia |
| | Florales | | Larentalia |
| May | Lemuria | | Sol Invictus |
| | Tiber | | |
| | Agonalia | | |
| | Tubilustrium | | |

*Source:* Matthew Bunson, *A Dictionary of the Roman Empire* (Oxford: Oxford University Press, 1995), 156.

(753 BCE). But the vast majority were annual ceremonies honoring a specific deity, expressing devotion and requesting blessing. During the imperial age many of these festivals, which were event based or simply deity oriented, became opportunities to venerate the emperor and pray for his rule to flourish. This makes sense; many people came to see the emperor as a bridge between the world of the gods and the world of mere mortals.

## "Io Saturnalia!"

We can return now to the question of how Romans saw time in general. Did they live life as a cycle of spring and fall, planting and harvesting? Or did they see time as a journey, coming from somewhere and going somewhere? Yes. We have several accounts of Roman history from ancient writers precisely because they wanted to recount the unfolding of the story of this great empire. And with this combination of cyclical and linear, Romans would have had much in common with Jews and Christians. But let's consider an aspect of time they did *not* have in common: eschatological hope. This was truly a Jewish-Christian innovation, which took linear chronology to a whole other level. Roman writers held out hope for the future of Rome, but they never came close to the kind of certainty that Christians had.

Let's talk about some of these histories of Rome penned by Roman writers. Livy wrote a massive account composed of 142 books (i.e., chapters), only a small portion of which has survived. But thankfully we have the early books where Livy explains *why* he wrote this history. He believed that people ought to know the past of their nation, to learn from the successes and failures of their leaders. Imitate what is best and for the good, and avoid what is wrong and harmful to oneself and others. Livy is clear about two things: first, the founding

116

## Excerpt from Gregory Aldrete, *Daily Life in the Roman City*

"Originally an agricultural festival held during the winter solstice, [Saturnalia] was meant particularly to honor the god Saturn, who was associated with grain and the growing of wheat. The Saturnalia initially was held just after the last wheat crop of the year was sown. Eventually the Romans settled on December 17 as the date to celebrate the Saturnalia, but as the festival grew in popularity, they kept adding days until, by the high empire, the Saturnalia was a full, weeklong holiday beginning on the 17th. The official component of the Saturnalia was December 17, when the senators performed a mass animal sacrifice at the temple of Saturn, and afterward there was a huge banquet to which everyone was invited. The rest of the week was taken up with non-stop parties and feasts. All shops, law courts, and schools were closed. Normal moral restraints were loosened and everyone was expected to engage in all forms of revelry and fun. This was the only time of year when people were legally allowed to gamble in public. Bands of revelers ran through the streets drinking and shouting '*Io Saturnalia!*'"[a] (see fig. 7.3 on p. 118)

a. Gregory S. Aldrete, *Daily Life in the Roman City: Rome, Pompeii, and Ostia* (Westport, CT: Greenwood, 2004), 119.

of Rome shows nobility, honor, wisdom, and strength; second, Rome has become a victim of its own success. Its wealth has made the people fat, lazy, and greedy.[4] A historian typically looks at time in a linear fashion (moving from one key event to the next); nevertheless Livy is clear that Rome's best days were far behind, and his writing endeavor was intended to remind a backsliding people of the nobility of their origins.

Another Roman historian, Dionysius of Halicarnassus (60 BCE–7 BCE), expressed a similar sentiment in his *Roman Antiquities*. Dionysius called the founders of Rome "godlike

Figure 7.3. *Saturnalia*, by Antoine-François Callet (1783)

men" who chose honor and hard work but says that the men of his own time were marked by pleasure and ease. So Dionysius desired that history would point back to the best of the past to inspire living up to the high morals and work ethic of the great ancestors.[5]

What can we say about a Roman view of time? It appears that many Romans believed in a *chronology of decline,* a continual slipping away from a once-great past that had become far removed from the present. In fact, both Greeks and Romans passed down a golden-age myth that perceived the current state of the world as a far cry from an idyllic era long past.[6] The Roman poet Virgil (70 BCE–19 BCE) longed for a *new* golden age for Rome, with a view toward the sturdy leadership of Octavian, who became Rome's first emperor (Caesar Augustus) beginning in 27 BCE. Virgil wrote, "Hail to you, Augustus Caesar, son of a god, who will once more establish the golden age amid the fields where Saturn once reigned."[7] This is quite a tribute, but very few other writers predicted a return of the golden age. Many desired great prosperity for Rome, but few imitated the optimism of Virgil.

## Judaism and "Covenantal Time"

Rabbi Jonathan Sacks argues that Jews have wrestled with two ways of looking at their own religious traditions. He gives an example from an ancient rabbinic debate. One rabbi, Shammai, bestowed a special honor to the holy Sabbath, and if he found a choice animal to eat, he would say, "Let this be for the Sabbath." Rabbi Hillel, on the other hand, honored the Sabbath but carried the philosophy "Blessed be the Lord day by day" (Ps. 68:20). Sacks explains that Shammai had a more linear view, seeing time as movement toward a destination. "Already from the beginning of a week, he was conscious of its end." But Hillel focused on the present: "Each day is a universe." Sacks sums up: "Each has its own challenge, its task, its response." So, which view is correct? Which one is orthodox? "Biblical"? Sacks sees the value in cyclical rhythms as we read Ecclesiastes' reflection on the rising and setting sun and the movement of the waters: "What has been will be again, what has been done will be done again."[8] This is not futility; we must be prepared for the natural repetitions of life. The priest knows this, faithfully offering sacrifices in keeping with Torah, according to the holy calendar.

But we see something else in the Jewish Scriptures as well, Sacks argues—"covenantal time," he calls it.[9] Because of sin—a power that corrupted God's good creation—the world was set off course almost immediately. But God made a plan and invested in a people, Israel. A covenant was formed, and divine promises were made. Now the countdown would begin for Israel to realize all its hopes. In a way, the Hebrew prophets were meant to hold Israel accountable to a God who would come through in the end. Sacks explains, "Knowing the previous chapters of the story, [the prophet] understands not only the present chapter but also where it is leading to. That is prophetic consciousness—time as narrative, time not as it is in nature but in history, or more specifically in covenant history, whose events are determined by free human choice but whose themes have been sent long in advance."[10]

Jews were probably not the first people to understand and live by the linear concept of time. But what seems to be true is that their devotion became fixated on the fulfillment of the covenantal promises of their God and that their cyclical rhythms of ritual and holiday, routine as they may have been, reinforced that eschatological narrative: one day things will finally become as they were meant to be from the beginning and will stay that way forever.

## Christianity and the Christ Era

The early Christians were obsessed with time. Not the question, What time is it? Anyone late for a meeting is bound to ask that question, whether in the ancient past or today. No, they dwelled on the question, Is it time yet? They were a people constantly looking forward. "Is the time right? Is time ready?" Their preferred language was "full," as in "fulfillment." They imagined time as if it were a container with fill markers on it, like a water bottle measuring milliliters. Because of Christianity's background in Jewish tradition, time was conceived of as being predetermined to reach eras of "fulfillment," time stages in the divine plan.[11] Mary Beard observes how odd Christians were among their peers for their lack of time orientation regarding feasts and festivals. Their minds were not on remembering to honor all the holy days but on just one time event—the time of the Messiah. Hence, Beard argues that Romans viewed time as polycentric, and Christians as monocentric. The Roman calendar tracked celebrations of many deities in view of a variety of legendary events. But the Christians narrowly concentrated their view of time on the Christ era.[12]

We can chart Christian time according to a strong binary, "before" and "after": "before the Christ era" and "the Christ era." This is represented well by Paul's statement to the Galatians: "When the fullness of time had come, God sent his Son, born of a woman, born under the law, in order to redeem those who were under the law, so that we might receive adoption as children" (Gal. 4:4–5). God was waiting until the right time to enact his plan of redemption, to kick off the Christ era. Given how the early Christians used fulfillment language, we can further break down this Christ era into segments: the incarnation, the gospel ministry of Jesus, the cross and resurrection, and the day of Christ.

*Time for God in the flesh.* The English word "incarnation" is a tribute to the Gospel of John, which narrates a time when the Word was in heaven and then "became flesh and lived among us" (John 1:14). This is the beginning of the "good news" of the fulfillment of the covenantal promises of Israel's God. And in fact the Gospel writers point to verses in Isaiah as a prophetic "spoiler" that foreshadowed salvation coming in the form of a baby king.

> The people who walked in darkness
> > have seen a great light;
> those who lived in a land of deep darkness—
> > on them light has shined. . . .

121

> For a child has been born for us,
>   a son given to us;
> authority rests upon his shoulders;
>   and he is named
> Wonderful Counselor, Mighty God,
>   Everlasting Father, Prince of Peace.
> His authority shall grow continually,
>   and there shall be endless peace
> for the throne of David and his kingdom.
>   He will establish and uphold it
> with justice and with righteousness
>   from this time onward and forevermore.
>       (Isa. 9:2, 6–7; cf. Matt. 1:23; 4:16)

No Hebrew person in Isaiah's time thought this prophecy would be fulfilled in Jesus Christ, the God-man, the Second Person of the Trinity. But it is worth recognizing that Israel's prophets kept faith and hope alive by pointing to a new era of history that would begin with a royal birth.

Another prophetic voice helps us understand Jewish anticipation of the transformative dawning of the new, messianic age. According to Luke, Mary (the mother of Jesus) was blessed with prophetic intuition as she carried this unique child in her womb. She sings her famous hymn we call the Magnificat:

> My soul magnifies the Lord,
>   and my spirit rejoices in God my Savior,
> for he has looked with favor on the lowliness of his
>     servant.
> Surely, from now on all generations will call me
>     blessed;
> for the Mighty One has done great things for me,
>   and holy is his name.
> His mercy is for those who fear him
>   from generation to generation.

He has shown strength with his arm;
  he has scattered the proud in the thoughts of their
    hearts.
He has brought down the powerful from their
    thrones,
  and lifted up the lowly;
he has filled the hungry with good things,
  and sent the rich away empty.
He has helped his servant Israel,
  in remembrance of his mercy,
according to the promise he made to our ancestors,
  to Abraham and to his descendants forever.
    (Luke 1:46–55)

Notice that Mary says nothing about the baby or the eventual adult king. Rather, she praises the inevitable *effects* that will be wrought by this new kingdom of God: the proud will be humbled, the people at the top will know what it is like to live at the bottom, those deprived of dignity and sustenance will have their fill, and the fat and spoiled will know want and need. God will act to right all the wrongs, raise up valleys, and flatten mountains. That is what this hope-filled era was all about. The incarnation was not just the beginning of a new season. It was the formation of a new world. The time had come.

*Time for the good news.* Truth be told, we know too little about Jesus's young life, what he did and said before he launched his public ministry. The focus of the Gospels is on the preaching and activity of Jesus and, of course, his death and resurrection. When Jesus kicks off his teaching tour in the Gospel of Mark, he says, "*The time is fulfilled*, and the kingdom of God has come near; repent, and believe in the good news" (1:15). The movement of time has reached a key marker; now the next stage in God's plan has been activated. Some scholars link this to a text like Daniel 7:22, where the prophet sees both the emergence of the "Ancient One" and the arrival of the time when the holy people gain possession of the kingdom.[13] It is instructive that in Luke's Gospel Jesus refers to the period of his ministry as the "time of your visitation from God" (19:44)—meaning that God is at work in Jesus, revealing his plan and will. This is a key moment in history for God's people to pay attention.

*Time to die.* In the Gospel of John, Jesus has a very keen sense of time. His internal clock is set to a certain definitive "hour." His actions are limited based on a particular moment that must pass. Even while he does ministry, he is aware of it. For example:

Jesus is apprehensive about doing a public miracle at the wedding in Cana, because his "hour" has not yet come (John 2:4).

Later on, Jesus is not able to be arrested; he evades getting into hot water with the authorities, because his "hour" has not yet come (7:30; 8:20).

When Jesus is about to be arrested, he confides in his disciples that the "hour" is near. He admits that his soul is troubled, but he knows that he was sent for this moment (12:27).

He will die, depart from this world, and go to the Father (13:1).

While many will see this crucifixion as a mark of shame, Jesus is convinced it will bring glory to the Father (17:1).

The special focus on Jesus's death, resurrection, and ascension had already become a central part of Christian belief and proclamation by the middle of the first century; as Paul writes to the Romans, "*At the right time* Christ died for the ungodly" (Rom. 5:6; cf. Heb. 10:12, 14).

It's worth mentioning that sometime in the first century Christians started observing a special day of worship, not on the last day of the week (Saturday, the traditional Jewish Sabbath), but on the first day (Sunday). This was called "the Lord's day" to commemorate the resurrection of the Messiah (Rev. 1:10). This is also referenced in the early Christian text known as the Didache, where believers are instructed to gather and break bread on the Lord's day (14.1). The one rhythmic tradition observed by all early Christians focused on the new beginning of the resurrection day. Michael Lipka adds that Easter (*pascha*) was the only annual festival celebrated by Christians in the first three centuries.[14]

*The "final" time.* Peter makes reference to "the final time," the *eschaton*, an era that has nothing new after it (1 Pet. 1:5, my trans.). This is variously expressed by early Christians as "the fullness of time" (Eph. 1:10), the second "manifestation of our Lord Jesus Christ" (1 Tim. 6:14), and the "time of universal restoration" (Acts 3:21). Paul also calls it the "day of Christ" (Phil. 1:10; 2:16) because on it the Messiah will oversee the final judgment. Christ will "set things right," as Hebrews puts it (Heb. 9:10).[15] Christians lived in eager anticipation of this final time, and their anticipation was imprinted on their liturgy with the ancient Aramaic word *maranatha*, "Come, Lord Jesus" (Rev. 22:20; cf. 1 Cor. 16:22).

*The "now" time.* We have charted the chain links of the time orientation of the early Christians. But it is worth asking how they saw the "now" time, the present in which they lived. Theologians are accustomed to calling this the "already-not yet," a time of fulfillment (looking back) and also a time of anticipation (looking ahead). They talk about making the most of time (Col. 4:5), as believers are called to be faithful in obedience while Christ is "away" and ready for when Christ returns. "The appointed time has grown short" (1 Cor. 7:29). Believers must be on guard because the devil wants to ruin their faith and "the days are evil" (Eph. 5:16). Paul gives us a glimpse of the urgency of Christian faithfulness in his call for the Roman churches to stay alert: "You know what time it is, how it is now the moment for you to wake from sleep. For salvation is nearer to us now than when we became believers" (Rom. 13:11). Christians must cast aside any form of evil and wear the armor of light: "Put on the Lord Jesus Christ, and make no provision for the flesh, to gratify its desires" (13:14).

## The Christian Sacrament of Hope

Christians from the beginning were obsessed with time—not the hour on the sundial but Jewish covenantal time, which grew into messianic time. They came to focus their time orientation on the key events of the appearance of Jesus Christ: his incarnation, his life, his death, his resurrection, his ascension—and then his return. The keeping of time became a kind of sacrament, reminding them of the gospel as good news and hope for the world.

# PART THREE

# How
# the First
# Christians
# Worshiped

# A Household of Faith

## The Family Practices
## of the Early Christians

Let us work for the good of all, especially for those who
belong to the household of faith.

St. Paul, Galatians 6:10

The early Christian writer named Minucius Felix (died
ca. 250 CE) published a defense of Christianity in the
second century CE. His work, called *Octavius*, presents
a back-and-forth between a pagan critic of Christianity named
Caecilius and a Christian named Octavius, with Felix acting
as narrator.* One of the many accusations that Caecilius hurls
against Christians concerns the secretive and subversive behavior of this dangerous sect.

*Some scholars think that Caecilius here is a fictional character used to represent
popular critiques of Christianity at the time.

129

Why is it not a thing to be lamented, that men . . . of reprobate, unlawful, and desperate faction, should rage against the gods? Who, having gathered together from the lowest dregs the more unskilled, and women, credulous and, by the facility of their sex, yielding, establish a herd of a profane conspiracy, which is leagued together by nightly meetings, and solemn fasts and inhuman meats . . . a people skulking and shunning the light, silent in public, but garrulous in corners. They despise temples as dead-houses, they reject the gods, they laugh at sacred things; wretched, they pity, if they are allowed, the priests.[1]

Caecilius goes on: These Christians have secret symbols and codes, and when they come together, they give in to lust masquerading as "love." They call each other "brother and sister," which means they willfully commit incest. Caecilius admits he knows none of this firsthand; he cannot observe their weird behavior *because* they are so secretive!

While Caecilius doesn't come right out and say it, he seems to point to the oddity of their assemblies taking place in private, in houses. Christians don't have temples and statues, which are out in the open. They meet early in the morning or late at night behind closed doors, doing who knows what. What are they hiding? Caecilius is very open to the rumors that this means Christians feast and party, which leads to sex parties. Proper Roman piety happens at set times and days, with overseeing priests and plenty of decorum. But these Christians are going wild under the cover of darkness. Caecilius mentions that whole families of men, women, and children come together to feast and get drunk and let desire and lust run wild.

He wonders aloud to Octavius,

Why do they endeavour with such pains to conceal and to cloak whatever they worship, since honourable things always rejoice in publicity, while crimes are kept secret? Why have they no altars, no temples, no acknowledged images? Why do

130

they never speak openly, never congregate freely, unless for the reason that what they adore and conceal is either worthy of punishment or something to be ashamed of? Moreover, whence or who is he, or where is the one God, solitary, desolate, whom no free people, no kingdoms, and not even Roman superstition,* have known?[2]

The upshot of Caecilius's argument is this: only guilty people hide, and these Christians are so deeply hidden that they must be the worst of all society. If what they have is so great, why is it such a well-kept secret?

Obviously, Christians then and now, and all throughout history, would be quick to refute Caecilius's accusations—even Caecilius admits this is hearsay, though he heard it a lot, I assume. But behind this gossip is some truth, especially that Christians did not have temples and cult statues and that they made it a habit and tradition of meeting in houses at mealtimes.

## The People Who Meet in Houses

Pliny the Younger (61–113 CE) was a Roman magistrate who was called on to investigate these strange Christians and report back to Emperor Trajan. He explains to Trajan that "they had met regularly before dawn on a fixed day to chant verses alternately among themselves in honour of Christ as if to a god, and also to bind themselves by oath, not for any criminal purpose, but to abstain from theft, robbery, and adultery, to commit no breach of trust and not to deny a deposit when called upon to restore it."[3] Pliny's understanding of Christian practice corresponds with what we find in the New Testament, especially the notion that Christians assembled on a regular basis. Now,

---

*"Roman superstition" meaning "fringe cults" in the empire that don't carry official approval.

it is helpful to know that weekly worship meetings were not a universal or even common practice in Roman religion. We have already mentioned Roman holidays, which were mandatory and functioned like festivals. But a small group coming together for worship and instruction was not the norm. There were two exceptions to this in the Roman world. First, you had Jews who gathered in synagogues for learning and prayer. Second, there were small organizations we call Greco-Roman voluntary associations, which met regularly for business, religious, and social purposes. But the Christians had this vast network of assemblies across the Roman Empire by the time of Trajan's reign (98–117 CE), and they coordinated, more or less, a worldwide common gathering day (Sunday). Jews, of course, gathered on their Sabbath day (Saturday), but Christians apparently gravitated toward Sunday to honor the new day of the resurrected Lord.

It can be demonstrated not only that Christians habitually gathered one day a week but that they met in houses by default.* In the book of Acts, when Peter escapes prison by divine intervention, he goes looking for his Christian friends, and where does he go first? "To the house of Mary, the mother of John whose other name was Mark, where many had gathered and were praying" (Acts 12:12). From Paul's letters, we know that "churches" (Christian assemblies) were associated with a particular leader, in many cases the household owner (in Roman terms, the *paterfamilias* or *materfamilias*).

> Greet Prisca and Aquila. . . . Greet also the church in their house. (Rom. 16:3, 5)

---

*"Houses" doesn't mean large, independent dwellings. These could have been the Roman equivalent of apartments, or perhaps something like a home workshop or a meeting room attached to a home. We will use the term "house" in a broad sense to refer to a home that may vary in size, type, and function. For a more nuanced discussion, see Edward Adams, *The Earliest Christian Meeting Places* (London: T&T Clark, 2013).

The churches of Asia send greetings. Aquila and Prisca, together with the church in their house, greet you warmly in the Lord. (1 Cor. 16:19)

Give my greetings to the brothers and sisters in Laodicea, and to Nympha and the church in her house. (Col. 4:15)

To Philemon our dear friend and co-worker, to Apphia our sister, to Archippus our fellow soldier, and to the church in your house. (Philem. 1–2)

Why did Christians meet in houses? Well, we might wonder, where else were they going to assemble? They could meet outside, in a park or a garden, but there would have been questions about comfort and privacy. They could have gathered in a business or a community space, but as we will discuss later in the chapter, the house facilitated an important part of their ritual worship: a shared meal. So houses made sense. But there was more to it than convenience and logistics. We will break our discussion down into three parts: (1) a new family, (2) household leadership, and (3) the transformative social table.

## A New Family

We noted already that Caecilius, the critic of Christianity, mentioned how weird it was that Christians called each other "brother" and "sister" and shared ritual kisses at night in the privacy of houses. You can see how rumors might spread, and people would naturally ask questions. But this tells us a lot about how Christians thought of each other—namely, as *family*. In the Roman world, family was the most important building block for society. As the family thrived, so did the whole empire. And the opposite was true: if the family was disorderly and chaotic, this would shake the very foundation of society. Many viewed the household as a microcosm of the empire and the empire as a macro-version of the household. This is well stated by ancient Jewish philosopher Philo of Alexandria: "A household is a city on a small and contracted scale, and the management of a household is a contracted kind of polity; so that a city may be called a large house, and the government of a city a widely spread [household] economy. . . . The manager of a household and the governor of a state are identical, though the multitude and magnitude of the things committed to their charge are different" (*On the Life of Joseph* 1.38, 39).[4]

The earliest Christians were intentionally deconstructing a Romanized approach to family and constructing a *new* family and household. This was dangerous business, fiddling with the building blocks of civilization, but this became the primary way Christians saw their relationship to one another. Now, that didn't mean they broke away from blood ties and abandoned their spouses. But their family in Christ was meant to take priority in shaping their identity, and this way of thinking started with Jesus.

We can begin with Jesus's own question about family in the Gospel of Matthew. Someone tells Jesus while he is teaching that his mother and brothers are trying to get closer to him. Jesus takes this simple remark and opens up a big can of worms about who counts as family: "Who is my mother, and who are my brothers? . . . Here are my mother and my brothers!" (12:48–49). Jesus is pointing to his disciples and explaining that "whoever does the will of my Father in heaven is my brother and sister and mother" (12:50). In the Gospel of John, a similar kind of family-shifting statement is made by Jesus after he has been resurrected. When Mary Magdalene realizes she is talking to Jesus, she wants to cling to him, but he tells her, "Do not hold on to me, because I have not yet ascended to the Father. But go to my brothers and say to them, 'I am ascending to my Father and your Father, to my God and your God'" (John 20:17). Jesus the Son has a natural connection to the heavenly Father that he wants to share with all who follow him, who abide in the Son.

Since Jesus talked about forming a new family, it was natural for the early churches to gather in homes and treat each other *as* family. This family-type behavior is reinforced in many early Christian texts in several ways. One of the titles most used of God is "Father," signaling the protective and caregiving nature of God and also the idea that all these people are equal children of one Father. Jesus is God's one true Son,[5] and all believers find their place in this new family *through* the sonship of Christ. Paul uses this imagery when writing to the Roman churches: "For those whom [God] foreknew he also predestined to be conformed to the image of his Son, in order that he might be the firstborn within a large family" (Rom. 8:29).

Jesus the Son is the living spiritual DNA link between believers and God the Father. He graciously opens up his sonship to include a massive new family. In Roman families, while there was a natural sense of care and concern for one another, there was also a tiered structure that involved different levels of importance for different members. Generally speaking, men were more important than women, older more important than younger, pure blood more privileged than half siblings, let alone slaves. Slaves were counted within households, but they did not "count" as people. They had no family name, no honor, no inheritance, no future; basically, they were living forms of property, much like cattle. But Christian writers like Paul ascribed dignity and honor to all within the household of faith, including slaves. The redemption made possible by Jesus the Son enables everyone to be included in God's family, with the same welcome status as Jesus himself, no more, no less; just as Jesus the true Son cried, "Abba! Father!" so any child of God can say the same through Jesus's privilege and the Spirit's power (Gal. 4:1–7). This is the context for Paul's famous equality statement: "As many of you as were baptized into Christ have clothed yourselves with Christ. There is no longer Jew or Greek, there is no longer slave or free, there is no longer male and female; for all of you are one in Christ Jesus. And if you belong to Christ, then you are Abraham's offspring, heir according to the promise" (3:28–29).

The social effect that this would have had on the Christian communities is massive. Joseph Hellerman explains that in the ancient world households held to certain standards and embodied a special ethos.[6] First, there was a strong sense of *commitment*. Families were there for each other through thick and thin. Second, they worked together as a *team*. Often, families were like small businesses, everyone having to play their part for the benefit of the whole. This would complement Paul's member/body language and imagery. Family members exercised their gifts and skills to support the whole household. Third, families *shared* resources and possessions. Real brothers and sisters would often share clothes, tools, furniture, and money, among other things. This is precisely the vision that is cast in the book of Acts about the way of the church, a sharing community where everyone pooled material resources for the common good (Acts 4:32–35). Finally, families *loved* each other. Sharing and working together was hard work, but it was not just business. It began, ended, and was carried out because of mutual affection and real concern for one another. Precisely when Paul detects that the Philippian church is showing fractures in their community, he prays for love (Phil. 1:9–11), which is what family is meant to reflect.

It may not have happened right away, but pretty quickly in the development of early Christianity, believers saw each other as family, and they met in homes to worship together and model generous community, worshiping the true God of home and world. But there were more reasons for the practice of household assembly. One of them was leadership.

## Household Leadership

Roger Gehring makes an interesting argument in his book *House Church and Mission*. His theory goes like this: The apostles preached and shared the good news of Jesus Christ with everyone, all kinds of people from least to greatest. But they made a strategic decision to invest in householders (i.e., leaders of households). Why? Because if householders became converts and advocates of Jesus and the gospel, they could provide stable and wise leadership to household and neighborhood communities. A good householder of a relatively large household (let's say fifty people, which includes biological family, paid staff, and slaves) probably had some education and would have already gained skills of management. This makes sense as we look at Paul's advice to Timothy about the role of overseer in the church. Such Christian leaders, Paul advises, ought to be faithful, self-controlled, wise, honorable, hospitable, good teachers, and careful with money, and they ought to model competent household management: "For if someone does not know how to manage his own household, how can he take care of God's church?" (1 Tim. 3:5).[7]

I think Gehring's theory is more than plausible, and this tells us a lot about why Christians were inclined to meet in houses. These Christian householders not only hosted gatherings but also were natural leaders in these Christian assemblies. For example, let's look at someone mentioned in 1 Corinthians: Stephanas. Paul mentions that Stephanas and his household were among the first converts to the faith in Achaia and that they dedicated themselves to ministry leadership (1 Cor. 16:15). This implies that Stephanas himself, a householder,

## Roman Household Religion

Romans made a distinction between public piety (honoring the
gods who protected the whole of
Roman life and society) and household devotion.[a] Three deities safe-
guarded the house and household.
Vesta, goddess of the hearth, represented the fiery heart of the home.
Then there were the Lares (singular
"Lar"; see fig. 8.1) and Penates (singular "Penus"); these were spirits or
sprites who, respectively, cared for family events and the household storehouse.
Various rooms of a Roman house would
have *lararia*, small shrines dedicated to the
Lares. Household members would pray to
the Lares on a regular basis for family bless-

Figure 8.1.
An ancient
Roman Lar
Luis García (Zaqarbal)/
Wikimedia Commons/
CC by SA 3.0, 2.5,
2.0, 1.0

ing and would express special devotion on occasions like the birth
of a child or when a family member was sick. One of the best pieces
of evidence for the role of the Lares in household religion comes
from Plautus's *Pot of Gold*, a fictional story in which a Lar plays
a key role. The stingy father of the house, Euclio, is hiding a pot
of gold, and his daughter Phaedria needs it for a dowry. The Lar
plays a role in changing the fate of this family to bless Phaedria,
who has been faithful to the Lar. Here is how the play begins:

> So that no one may wonder who I am, I will put it briefly: I am
> the *Lar familiaris* of the house out of which you have just seen me
> come. I have possessed and watched over this house for many years
> now, already for the father and the grandfather of the man who
> lives in it now. . . . He [the present owner] has only one daughter.
> She sacrifices incense or wine to me every day, or prays in some
> way to me again and again, decorating me with garlands.[b]

What did Christians do with these shrines devoted to the
Lares and Penates as part of their past? We can assume that most

Christians took seriously the apostolic instruction to renounce idols (1 Thess. 1:9–10) and that they removed *lararia*. John Barclay finds a possible clue in Romans 14:6 for how Christians turned their household devotion away from the Lares and toward Christ alone: "Those who eat, eat in honor of the Lord, since they give thanks to God."[c] Normally, one would honor the Lares and Penates for family provisions. But Christians did all things, inside the house and outside, for the sake of the Lord Jesus Christ. This would have been somewhat new territory for Gentiles who grew up venerating Lares and Penates as household spirits. But there would have been some sense of peace as well, knowing that Jesus Christ was lord of *all*, no matter what and no matter where.

The Christian writer Tertullian (160 CE–ca. 220 CE) came out strongly against idols in his defense of Christianity, critiquing Romans in general for the foolish veneration of mere statues, inside and outside the home. In his text *Apologies* (meaning "Defense"), he mentions the household Lares and the hypocrisy of many Romans who extend to them absolute power and yet sometimes treat the statues flippantly, "pawning them, selling them, or changing them" or even melting metal ones into pans or ladles.[d]

a. See Cicero, *On the Laws* 2.19–22, and the discussion in Mary Beard, John North, and Simon R. F. Price, *Religions of Rome* (Cambridge: Cambridge University Press, 1998), 2:353.

b. As quoted in Hans-Josef Klauck, *The Religious Context of Early Christianity: A Guide to the Graeco-Roman Religions* (Edinburgh: T&T Clark, 2000), 60.

c. John M. G. Barclay, "The Family as the Bearer of Religion in Judaism and Early Christianity," in *Constructing Early Christian Families*, ed. Halvor Moxnes (London: Routledge, 1997), 76.

d. Tertullian, *Apologetical Works*, The Fathers of the Church 10, trans. R. Arbesmann, E. J. Daly, and E. Quain (Washington, DC: Catholic University Press, 1950), 43.

was a key leader of a house church that met in his home. This is further reinforced by Paul's statement at the beginning of the letter that he himself baptized Stephanas, reflecting the apostle's personal investment in Stephanas's training for leadership. Likewise, Paul names another Christian called Gaius, who also probably hosted an assembly in his house (Rom. 16:23) and who was another one of the very few people whom

Paul baptized himself. And likewise for Crispus (1 Cor. 1:14; cf. Acts 18:8).

The leadership of householders in the Christian gatherings probably gave the worship times a strong sense of family community. Believers were not filled with dread as they prayed and honored their deity, seeking appeasement. They walked into a community of love and belonging. This was a *family* meeting. And one regular tradition of that family time was sharing a meal.

## The Transformative Social Table

A common tradition in Roman society was holding dinner parties, based on the Greek *symposium*, which brought together not only family but also neighbors and various friends and associates. While this event involved food and drink, it would be a mistake to consider eating to be the focus. Rather, it was a social event that reflected the host's social values and reminded those present (and absent) where they sat on the spectrum of importance. Warren Carter explains that these meals "underlined social stratification. Guests were seated according to different quantities and qualities of food in different quality tableware."[8] The ancient philosopher Plutarch explains that the goal of investing in one of these often lavish dinner parties is not just to eat and drink but to be *seen* eating and drinking with certain people.[9]

In the house's *triclinium* (dining room), the most privileged guests would recline closest to the food. Less important guests would be seated further away, and women and children, if present, would be positioned even further from the food. Plutarch describes these house-party banquets as "a spectacle and a show,"[10] with more important guests being given closer viewing of the entertainment (like singers, musicians, and dancers), proximity to the delicious smells, and service that would ensure the food was still warm. Sometimes the privileges were so formalized that certain special seats were permanently reserved for guests of honor. While this tiered experience was most overt and noticeable among the elite,[11] it was also the norm among commoners. This reflects the essence of Romanness, a constant reinforcement of social values in Roman culture: social life was set up as a pyramid of power. There were a precious few "haves" and a lot of "have-nots," and there was no use in pretending that everyone was equal.*

Jesus did things quite differently and paved the way for a new social ethos, which could and had to be demonstrated at the dinner table. In fact, it was a common criticism of Jesus by his contemporaries that he openly shared the social table with "tax collectors and sinners" (Matt. 9:11; Mark 2:16; see also Luke 15:2). Luke tells the story of Jesus offending a Pharisee who hosts him for dinner. A stranger, a woman, makes her way into the house and washes Jesus's feet with her tears and covers them in expensive ointment. With even a basic understanding of Roman dinner etiquette, it is clear that this woman breaks major social boundaries. Not only does Jesus ignore this infringement, but he commends her for her love and care for him. And then Jesus turns the tables on Simon, his host: "I entered your house; you gave me no water for my feet, but she has bathed my feet with her tears and dried them with her hair. You gave me no kiss, but from the time I came in she has not stopped kissing my feet. You did not anoint my head with oil, but she has anointed my feet with ointment" (Luke 7:44–47). When I heard this story as a teenager, I just assumed that Simon, in his excitement about having Jesus over, forgot these hospitality gestures. But the more I learn about how these dinners sent signals of status and importance, I can't help but think Simon was purposefully putting Jesus in his place as an

---

*See chap. 11 on Christian values of equality and status-leveling.

inferior. Jesus cuts through the social games and says in effect, "This woman wants to be a caring host, but you (Simon) want to be an important host."

The point Jesus is making to Simon the Pharisee is reinforced in Jesus's parable of the dinner party. A certain man, Jesus teaches, plans a big party and invites his friends and associates. A slave goes out with personal invitations. One by one, each guest makes some excuse for why they can't be there. Let's say he invites eight couples, and each one thinks they are too good for this man; they want to remind him he is not that important to them. So, what does he do? He tells his slave to forget the invitations and go out to the streets and bring in the poor, the blind, and the lame—the people at the very bottom of society. And rather than host just a dozen of his supposed friends, he tells his slave to fill up his whole house with anyone and everyone who wants to taste his fine cuisine (Luke 14:15–24).

It's hard for us to appreciate just how unusual a decision this would be. In order to "translate" Jesus's parable into Western society, we might think of it as a fancy fundraiser dinner event. You make lots of preparations, decorate the house, make elaborate and expensive invitations, and then you invite all your friends and associates. And imagine that every single one of them sends you the signal that they are too busy and important to come to your little gathering. So what do you do then? You take all those fancy cupcakes and the chocolate-fondue fountain and the cedar-plank salmon and the champagne, and you go out into the streets and hand these delicacies to any stranger nearby, including a child riding a tricycle, some homeless people, and an immigrant street vendor. What an odd thing to do, right?

Jesus's parable is a response to his anger at how guests at a dinner he is attending fought over the seats of honor (Luke 14:7). He turns this occasion into a teaching moment, saying in essence, "Don't push and shove your way into the spotlight, but choose the lowest place, because God's kingdom works differently than mortal kingdoms, 'For all who exalt themselves will be humbled, and those who humble themselves will be exalted'" (14:10–11).

But old habits die hard, and we find in some Christian churches of the first century that Jesus's message was difficult to swallow. We find a clear case in the Corinthian church. Paul chastises them for turning the sacred Lord's Supper meal into a competitive dinner party: "When you come together, it is not really to eat the Lord's supper. For when the time comes to eat, each of you goes ahead with your own supper, and one goes hungry and another becomes drunk. What! Do you not have homes to eat and drink in? Or do you show contempt for the church of God and humiliate those who have nothing?" (1 Cor. 11:20–22).

Paul warns them that they must learn how to discern "the body," the church as a living organism that must live in unity rather than rivalry (1 Cor. 11:29). "So then, my brothers and sisters, when you come together to eat, wait for one another. If you are hungry, eat at home, so that when you come together, it will not be for your condemnation" (11:33–34). It is no coincidence that he calls them "brothers and sisters" here. Paul is reinforcing the family identity of this community. Family shares. Family participates for the sake of the whole.

The Corinthian church is evidence that not all churches lived out Jesus's vision of status indifference. Not all churches let their new family identity take root. But the ideal was that those who willingly entered this community would join a special household of God. This would be unlike any other kind of household they knew. No one was of more importance or lesser importance in this family. Because of the invitation of Jesus the Son, each participant was simply "brother" or "sister." That cast a bold vision that would have been powerfully compelling, especially to "the least of these" (Matt. 25:40).

# A Priest-God
# and a Priestly People

## Church as a Liturgical Community

Let yourselves be built into a spiritual house, to be a holy
priesthood, to offer spiritual sacrifices acceptable to God
through Jesus Christ.

St. Peter, 1 Peter 2:5

I n the previous chapter, we began with the critic Caecilius's
concerns with the Christians. Most notably, it seemed to
many that Christians rejected Roman piety and devotion.
They treated temples as "dead-houses," mocked and scorned
sacred rituals, denied the gods, and pitied the priests, since
they had no material sacrifices to consecrate. We haven't yet
had a chance to talk about priests, but it is important to know
just how vital they were for Roman society. If priority number
one for Romans was maintaining the *pax deorum*, peace with

the gods, you needed specialists who could properly communicate with and appease the divine.

There is a made-to-order pizza place near my house. You go in, tell them what toppings you want, and they assemble the pizza right in front of you and throw it into the brick oven. Why don't customers just DIY it? Why can't I just walk in, make my own pizza, and throw it in the brick oven? Presumably because it's dangerous, and we leave it to the trained professionals so that no one gets hurt. These pizza specialists know how to avoid cross-contamination, they know in what order the toppings should go onto a pizza, and perhaps most important of all, they have special equipment that ensures they don't get burned by that blazing furnace that makes perfectly bubbling cheese and crispy-but-not-burned crust. Similarly, Roman priests were mediators, religious professionals who converted the people's worship into something suitable for the divine, and delivered something from the divine realm safely back to mortals.

But these Christians? They didn't have priests, certainly nothing like the Roman ones. You can search the whole New Testament, and you won't find a single reference to a Christian priest. You may find a Jewish priest of the temple who became a follower of Jesus, but he would not have functioned as a priest in a Christian assembly. It's hard for us today to wrap our minds around how odd and dangerous this would seem to Romans. Every religion, including Jewish religion, had priests. But you would search in vain for a priest to lead cultic practices in Christian meetings of worship in the first century.

In the late nineteenth and early twentieth centuries, scholars unearthed a heap of ancient documents in the city of Oxyrhynchus, Egypt (about one hundred miles south of Cairo). From this mass of business documents, sales receipts, and personal letters, we gain rich insight into life in the Greco-Roman world. In fact, it is one of the best sources for understanding early Christianity, as a number of Christian letters and texts were discovered in the remains. The Princeton scholar AnneMarie Luijendijk has analyzed materials dating from between 250 and 400 CE in order to understand leadership and institutional dynamics of early Christian churches. Her findings are fascinating and insightful.[1] She found about thirty total references to Christian leadership titles. The term "bishop" (*episkopos*, "overseer") was the most common, and there were a variety of titles that appeared less frequently.

One noticeable absence is the term "priest."* These texts name no priest or priesthood, no Levite or cult assistant of any kind. In fact, Luijendijk observes that the preferred leadership titles for Christians tended to come from the world of government and politics (like *leitourgos*, "public servant") rather than traditional religion. Ancient priests were, almost literally, gatekeepers for interaction with the divine realm, and many would assume that without them there would be religious anarchy. Priests are keepers of the *pax*, otherwise the wrath of the gods is inevitable!

It is not difficult to figure out, from Christians' unusual way of thinking about religion, why they didn't have priests. We will get to that later. For now, it helps to paint a picture of the kinds of priests that populated the Roman world. That way we can see how early Christian writers were reacting to, responding to, and deviating from the religious norms of society.

**Christian Leadership Titles from Oxyrhynchus Texts**

| Title | Number of Occurrences |
|---|---|
| Bishop/overseer | 11 |
| Monk | 5 |
| Presbyter/elder | 4 |
| Nun | 4 |
| Reader | 4 |
| Deacon | 1 |

*Source:* AnneMarie Luijendijk, "On and Beyond Duty: Christian Clergy at Oxyrhynchus (c. 250–400)," in *Beyond Priesthood: Religious Entrepreneurs and Innovators in the Imperial Era*, ed. Richard L. Godon, Jörg Rüpke, and Georgia Petridou (New York: de Gruyter, 2017), 106.

*While the term "priest" (*hiereus*) was not used by Christians in any official or technical capacity, we can sometimes see priestly language used as a metaphor for certain leadership functions. And our modern English term "priest" derives from the Greek term *presbyteros*, which typically refers to an elder but sometimes indicates a professional religious leader.

## Judaism and the Jewish Priesthood

According to Israel's tradition, when God freed his people from Egypt, he instituted a hereditary priesthood through Aaron, the brother of Moses (Exod. 28). These men would be marked out as holy to the Lord, and they would play a special role in keeping Israel pure. Eventually, their service was focused on the Jerusalem temple. The first temple was destroyed in 586 BCE by the Neo-Babylonian Empire. But a second temple was built, the one that Jesus and his disciples would have visited (see fig. 9.1).

While priesthood was hereditary, the twenty thousand priests serving the Jewish temple did not all live in Jerusalem, and their priestly work was not their full-time job.[2] According to 1 Chronicles 24, there were twenty-four divisions of priests, and they would travel to the temple for a period of duty and service. Each division would have served about two weeks per year and also supported large festivals.[3] For the common priest, this was not a lucrative role. The vast majority of priests had day jobs when they were not needed in temple service. Many served in their own towns as teachers, scholars, scribes, local magistrates, and judges.[4] Some may have helped to make ends meet by doing manual labor.[5]

When it came to temple service, Jewish priests performed a variety of tasks, but in practice they had one main job: handling meat sacrifices. As Robert Kugler explains, "The main task of priests was expert butchery: slaughtering animals, flaying them, cutting up the meat and distributing it, sprinkling and pouring blood on and around the altar, and putting fat and fatty pieces of meat on the altar. In most cases, the priests ate most of the meat, though in some sacrifices the worshiper who brought the animals received most of it."[6] They were also inspectors of offerings, ensuring that sacrifices were whole and unblemished and were given according to Scripture and

Ariely/Wikimedia Commons/CC by 3.0

**Figure 9.1.** The second Jewish temple. Model in the Israel Museum.

tradition. Priests didn't give sermons or schedule marriage-counseling sessions. They were cult technicians, specializing in processing sacrifices that were pleasing to the Lord.

While it is true that the vast majority of those twenty thousand priests were common people, some had more power and status. An obvious example is the Jewish high priest. While technically the high priest was a hereditary role, that was not always the case after Jews returned to their land from exile in Babylon. As the second temple was built, the high priest became a more prominent *political* figure in Israel, and eventually, under Roman rule, the high priesthood became more of a political appointment. This explains why the high priest played such a prominent role in Jesus's final week.

The New Testament makes frequent reference to "chief priests," people who appear to be aristocrats, a power class in Judea.[7] N. T. Wright describes them as a kind of "permanent secretariat, based in Jerusalem, wielding considerable power.

They belonged to a small group of families, tight-knit and inbred, who seem on several occasions to have engaged in serious factional disputes among themselves."[8] The phenomenon we see here, with politically interested and ambitious aristocratic Jewish priests, was probably influenced by the nature of priesthood in Roman religion.

## Priesthood in Roman Religion

Outside of Judaism, religious cults in the Roman world had two kinds of priests. Some were private priests who served in local cult rituals; imagine hiring someone to perform religious ceremonies at a wedding or at an ancestral holiday. These kinds of private priests were all around but were neither wealthy nor high class in most cases.[9] They performed a local service for non-state cults.

The more prominent cultural role in the Roman world was held by official state priests. These positions went to elite families of the senatorial class. Many such priests were politicians who were chosen to preside over public cult ceremonies.[10] Men competed for these priesthood positions, not because they were spiritual or wanted to serve the people, but because it gave them public recognition and social capital.[11]

There was an official pontifical college of sorts that was led by the *pontifex maximus* ("supreme priest"), the emperor himself. The college had four categories of priests.

> Pontiffs (literally "bridge-builders"). These leaders served as advisers and consultants on the administrative level, giving counsel on all matters related to keeping peace with the gods.
> Augurs (omen experts).[12] These were experts in announcing and interpreting omens and "auspices," which were observations of bird movement patterns. This was an

age-old tradition going back to the founders of Rome, Romulus and Remus. As legend tells it, Romulus and Remus decided where to build Rome with the guidance of the auspices. So, as the historian Livy explains, it was long decided that "no action was ever undertaken, in the field or at home, unless the auspices had been consulted: assemblies of people, war levies, great affairs of state—all would be put off if the birds withheld their approval."[13]

Fetials (martial priests). Fetials aided Rome in war duties such as making formal declarations of war and forming and abiding by treaties.[14] Therefore, they were as important for diplomatic reasons as they were for performing war-related rituals.

Quindecimviri[15] (literally "The Fifteen"). These fifteen priests were in charge of guarding the sacred literature known as the Sibylline Books, texts that were consulted as needed by the Senate when they looked to ancient prophecy for guidance.

As you can see, the work of Roman priests had little to do—actually *nothing* to do—with bettering the "spiritual lives" of individuals. The state cult was bound up with war, power, and politics that aimed at protecting and increasing Rome's greatness, and specifically the supremacy of the emperor in the imperial era. The following sums up the situation aptly:

[Roman] priests were not necessarily men of exceptional piety or believed to be endowed with special psychic or clairvoyant powers. They were, rather, men of learning, political experience, and high social rank who did not form any professional priestly class, even though they did have to come from certain *gentes* [social classes]. Their wealth enabled them to perform their priestly duties without financial reward. Some had been magistrates before becoming priests; some were priests and

Figure 9.2. *The Sacrifice of Vestal,* by Alessandro Marchesini (1710s). An eighteenth-century depiction of the Vestal Virgins.

magistrates simultaneously; and many were members of the senate. The chief qualification for holding a priesthood was the right pedigree as well as an exact knowledge of religious tradition, of divine law, and of correct ritual and ceremonial procedure.[16]

Last but not least, we need to mention the Vestal Virgins of Rome. These women served as priestesses of the goddess Vesta, and their prime duty was to keep the perpetual fire burning in the Temple of Vesta (see fig. 9.2). This represented the security of Rome, a kind of beating heart of the empire. These women served their duties for thirty years, during which time they had to maintain chastity and singleness. They were a unique group in Roman society, emancipated from their household and independent of any man. As assistants to the great goddess Vesta, they also enjoyed elevated status and social power similar to Roman senators and power-wielding Roman priests.

## A Priestless Religion?

If a visitor to a first-century church spent enough time with Christians, they would naturally wonder, *Where are their priests?* Priests were gatekeepers and go-betweens, experts negotiating between two parties (gods and mortals). And their work was notoriously dangerous. Priests often played the role of representing the people before the gods, and if the gods were offended, the priests might pay the ultimate price. (The Greek and Roman gods didn't believe in the expression "Don't kill the messenger.")

Jewish priests also had to be careful not to offend their God as they carried out their work. Their duties must be carried out according to a certain standard of purity and holiness. The ancient Jewish philosopher Philo of Alexandria offers an extended reflection on the grand work of the Jewish high priest.[17] Just like a spotless sacrifice, he must be perfect and blameless before God. He must be wise in sacred matters. The high priest, in Philo's mind, plays a unique role among all humanity. He is not a god, but he is higher than any mortal. He lives in the space between the two, performing mediation. So, how is it possible that these Christians don't have priests?

The early Christian text that seems to reflect the most on this oddity is the book of Hebrews, where Jesus himself is portrayed as a singular, unique, and final high priest. Because of Jesus, no traditional human priest is needed again. He is the perfect mediator and go-between. Several important things are affirmed about Jesus's priesthood in Hebrews.

*A priest from above.* While a priest is normally selected from among common humans and elevated (through consecration) to holy priesthood, in the case of Jesus it is the other way around. He came from heaven to become like mortals (Heb. 2:17). This notion is unprecedented in the ancient world. Yes,

153

gods might disguise themselves as humans to provide some aid or service, but to become human "in every respect" (2:17) is unexpected and even a bit absurd. What god would take that risk? Who would lower themselves in that way? But Jesus was simply following the calling and commission of the Father (3:1), standing ready to do whatever it took to complete the divine mission of redemption.

*A sympathetic priest.* Hebrews makes it clear that a regular, human priest can sympathize with the need for human atonement, as he represents his needy people before God. Jesus, the Son of God, knew no sin but made himself vulnerable to human temptation and weakness. This makes him all the more approachable, compassionate, and tenderhearted (Heb. 5:1–7).

*Eternal intercession.* Hebrews observes that priests in former times did as much as they could within the limitations of their mortality. But Jesus, Son of God, is able to pray and intercede for humans forever (Heb. 7:23–25).

*Self-sacrifice ending all material sacrifice.* Hebrews recognizes the end of the sacrificial requirement of worship—though not because it was meaningless. God gave the system to his people for a reason. But Jesus's world-transforming death was a perfect offering for the sake of human sin, once for all (Heb. 7:26–28; 9:11–13; 10:11–13). Through this, Jesus as the great priest has opened up "the new and living way" to approach and experience God (10:20).

Because Christians conceived of Jesus carrying out his high-priestly duties *in heaven*, how did believers imagine their devotion to God *on earth*? Who aided them in their worship? They appeared to rely on two sources: the Holy Spirit and each other. As for the Spirit, we can turn to Romans 8 to see how Paul sees the matter. He explains to the Romans that the Spirit is a kind of built-in mediator (priest), constantly fostering a relationship with God from within the human spirit: "The Spirit helps us in our weakness; for we do not know how to pray as we ought, but that very Spirit intercedes with sighs too deep for words. And God, who searches the heart, knows what is the mind of the Spirit, because the Spirit intercedes for the saints according to the will of God" (8:26–27).

This intercession functions as a kind of spiritual "autocomplete" in the conversation with God. Sometimes the Spirit knows what to say better than the believer does in the moment, and yet those words still capture the human heart. The Spirit has the agency and access, in the most vulnerable moments, to instantaneously transport believers to the close presence of God, calling out *"Abba* (Father)!" (Rom. 8:15). In that moment, believers are not just humble supplicants but beloved children of the most high God, brothers and sisters of Jesus the Son who are welcome in the presence of the divine parent.

We've talked about certain oddities of early Christianity as religious "technological innovations," such as the idea that you don't need to go to a temple or sacred location to "connect" with God; Christians could worship and interface with God safely and directly *anywhere*, kind of like the jump from landlines to mobile phones (see chap. 5). Well, it's hard for us moderns to understand this incredible phenomenon of having no professional priests. I want to use another modern analogy: eyesight.* When I was a kid, I had glasses, like many other children and adults. Sometimes I bent them, sometimes I broke them, sometimes I lost them. But like them or not, I needed them to see. In middle school I got contact lenses. What an amazing invention! You can't lose them as easily, and nobody is going to step on them or sit on them. But there's a downside: they are expensive, and there is a risk of eye infection without daily hygienic care of the lenses. But for me the real life-transforming experience was getting laser eye surgery to correct my vision. Imagine, for seven centuries about half the

*My dad is an eye surgeon, so he would be really proud of this illustration.

human population wore glasses. For most of that period, you didn't have a choice. If you wanted to see, you needed glasses. And then—*poof*—no more glasses. You can just . . . *see*. This would have been absolutely unfathomable to people in the thirteenth or fourteenth century or even most of the twentieth century. You have a doctor literally burn your eyeballs with a laser, and a few days later you can see the world clearly without glasses or contact lenses. A permanent problem fixed with a permanent solution. *Amazing*.

This captures, I hope, something of the awe-inducing phenomenon of Christians worshiping without priests. Now, Jewish synagogues did not require priests. These were worship settings with teaching and veneration, so you *could* honor God without a priest on hand in Jewish communities.[18] But to have *no priests at all*, to believe that Jesus ended sacrifice once for all and the Spirit "closed the gap," as it were, would have left people feeling uncomfortable, like someone trying to adjust their glasses and realizing they're not wearing any.

## The Worship Practices of the Early Christians

In one sense, Christians did not have priests who mediated their worship with God; that seems to be true formally. But, in another sense, they thought of themselves as a whole priesthood, a priest-people. In 1 Peter, Christians are described as individual stones that come together to form a "spiritual house," or a group of people who form a "holy priesthood, to offer spiritual sacrifices acceptable to God through Jesus Christ" (1 Pet. 2:5; cf. 2:9). Similarly, in the book of Revelation, there is a vision for the church as a kingdom of priests who live to serve God (Rev. 1:6; 5:10; 20:6).

*Baptism, a ritual of consecration.* What we call Christian baptism is never fully explained in the New Testament in terms of its origins and exact purposes. But we know it was an initiation rite that signaled inclusion in the social body and commitment and devotion to this particular deity. Paul refers to baptism as identification with the burial and death of Christ (going into the water) and Christ's resurrection and glory (coming out of the water), whereby the believer now lives a new life (Rom. 6:3–4; Col. 2:12). This is also a unifying ritual where Christians become one by the one Spirit of God (1 Cor. 12:13; Eph. 4:5). But we can also see how baptism is a consecration of each believer as a priest, giving them direct access to God, with no mediators, barriers, go-betweens, or red tape. Paul writes to the Corinthians, "You were washed, you were *consecrated*, you were made right with God in the name of the Lord Jesus Christ and in the Spirit of our God" (1 Cor. 6:11, my trans.). This almost feels like the kind of declaration that would happen at baptism, a purification ritual that sets each Christian apart as holy before God, consecrated to divine service. Just like the Vestal Virgins of Rome, who were consecrated for sacred service of the goddess Vesta, called to purity, and given great privileges and status. But in the case of Christians, it is not a select few who were consecrated but *all*.

*A whole-life "sacrifice."* When we use the language of "worship practices" in the Christian tradition, it is natural to think and talk about musical performance and hymn singing. And there are certainly times when the New Testament writers reference singing as an expression of praise to God (1 Cor. 14:15; Eph. 5:19; Col. 3:16). But the heart of Christian worship can best be seen in Romans 12:1–2: "Present your bodies as a living sacrifice, holy and acceptable to God, which is your spiritual worship. Do not be conformed to this world, but be transformed by the renewing of your minds, so that you may discern what is the will of God—what is good and acceptable and perfect." This idea goes far above the expectations of Roman religion. Roman people recognized that inhabitants ought to be respectful to the gods in order to secure the *pax deorum,* but to become living sacrifices would be a paradox that was difficult to grasp. But Romans 12:1–2 reinforces the Christian's baptism, a ritual of consecration to the Lord where believers are like both priests and sacrifices, offering themselves completely to God with nothing left over.

I am sure Christians viewed their singing and verbal praise as forms of sacrifice to God, but the metaphorical language of sacrifice was also used for service toward one another. For example, Hebrews mentions that doing good to others and sharing with them is a sacrifice pleasing to God (Heb. 13:16). Paul thanks the Philippians for their gifts of aid and support that they sent to him while he was in prison. He calls these gifts (we can guess of food, salves and oils, clothing, blankets, and writing supplies) "a fragrant offering, a sacrifice acceptable and pleasing to God" (Phil. 4:18). These were tangible examples of what it meant to be a living sacrifice, to give to others as an offering to the Lord.

*The worship practice of prayer.* If a first-century Roman were to stumble on a collection of early Christian writings (something like the canon of New Testament writings) and thumbed through it looking for patterns of religious practice, the most mentioned feature they would notice, I propose, is prayer. Nearly all the New Testament writers talk about prayer, and multiple writers make it appear that Christians were praying all the time, hence Paul's own command for the Thessalonians to "pray without ceasing" (1 Thess. 5:17). Jews, of course, practiced frequent prayer. In fact, Jesus (a devout Jew) affirmed that the revered Jerusalem temple was designed to be a house of prayer (Matt. 21:13).

As the church formed, according to the book of Acts, Christians made a conscious decision to devote "themselves to the apostles' teaching and Christian fellowship, to the breaking of bread and the prayers" (Acts 2:42). As needs arose in the community, the Twelve appointed additional leaders to distribute food so that the apostles could focus on teaching and prayer

(6:4). And Paul repeatedly emphasizes constant and passionate prayer (Rom. 12:12; Eph. 6:18; Col. 4:2). Romans looked at Jews and Christians with suspicion in part because of this obsession with prayer. This seemed overboard, religious zeal that lacked decorum. Now, of course, Roman people prayed. For example, they prayed regularly to their household gods, the Lares. And they went to temples and festivals and prayed. But these Christians—they took prayer to a whole other level. Romans would have wondered, *How can you pray without ceasing? Don't you have other things to do?*

I think the idea behind the Christian passion for prayer is a suffusing of life with the presence of God. Romans believed that the gods could appear anywhere if they wanted to, but under normal circumstances you went to a sacred hotspot (like a temple) and connected with the divine through time-honored rituals and formal prayers.

Jews, again, were a people of prayer, and they were not restricted from praying outside the temple—they could pray anytime, in any place—but there was a notion that divine glory was concentrated in a special way in the temple. We can look at Psalm 84 for a good example of how an Israelite worshiper processed this. The leader of the Korahites expresses a longing to be in the temple:

> Happy are those who live in your house,
>     ever singing your praise. (84:4)

A day in the temple courts is far better than a thousand days in any other place. The psalmist would rather be a temple doorkeeper than anywhere else in the world, just to be close to God (84:10–11).

The early Christians treated Israel's Scriptures, like this psalm, as sacred, but they came to see the divine presence in a different way. Christians could go no place where they were closer to the presence of the Lord, because they believed God's Spirit lived within them. There was a longing to know God in a deeper way that could happen only when the gospel work was complete, but even in the meantime there were no boundaries to divine communication and no rules or regulations for prayer. Each person had equal and unhindered access to God at all times, experiencing priestlike privileges.

## Participating in the Priesthood of Jesus Christ

Early in this chapter we looked at Luijendijk's research on what Christian leadership looked like according to the Oxyrhynchus papyri. We conclude this chapter with one final insight from her essay. When analyzing religious discourse across all Greco-Roman religions in the papyri from between 250 and 400 CE, Luijendijk noticed that prior to 250 it was common to see the language of priest/priesthood used for Roman cult officials (e.g., priests to Jupiter or Apollo). But between 250 and 350 CE we see a decline in occurrences of the word "priest" for such Roman offices. What Luijendijk is pointing to is the influence of Christianity on the Roman world, which led to Roman religion declining and the offices and language of priesthood disappearing. "A sea change has occurred in less than one hundred years."[19]

Some Christian traditions today use the category of "priest" for Christian leadership or service (Catholic, Anglican, Orthodox). We don't have the space to explore how these traditions view the nature of priesthood as a personal calling. But what appears to be shared across these traditions is the notion that any such human priests do not serve with their own independent agency but instead "priestify" as an extension of the unique priesthood of Jesus Christ. They become living channels or extensions of Jesus's unique agency as the living bridge between heaven and earth.

160

# How
the First
Christians
Lived

# Dangerous Contact

## Becoming Godlike

Our Lord Jesus Christ, the Word of God, of his boundless love, became what we are that he might make us what he himself is.

Irenaeus, *Against Heresies* 5, trans. John Anthony McGuckin, *We Believe in One Lord Jesus Christ*

Roman religion in general recognized that the gods deserved obedience and veneration, but it was dangerous and unwise to try to get *too* close to the divine. If the gods are like celestial masters and humans like slaves, it makes sense to keep a safe distance, pay your respect at arm's length, and stay out of their way. You might memorize excerpts of Homer and Virgil, and you might take trips to see the grand temples and statues across the land. There were ways to familiarize yourself more with the great and heavenly gods. But most people had no interest in communing with the divine.

That would be as sensible as sticking your head in the mouth of a lion to get a better look!

And yet we do find pockets of interest in what it meant to be close to the gods and to be like the gods in one way or another. An important religious phenomenon of the Greco-Roman world involved something called mystery cults.[1] These cults were not part of the public, state *religio*. This wasn't about maintaining peace with the gods to secure civic prosperity. These mystery cults involved a personal desire to commune with a deity and enjoy some benefits of their powers and knowledge. When early Christianity emerged and grew in the late first century, it had features that overlapped with these mystery cults, such that it could be mistaken for one. We will see how the Christians differed from mystery cults in several ways (including the Christian emphasis on moral purity), but what they had in common was a hunger for experiencing the divine.

## Greco-Roman Mystery Cults

First things first. Why are they called "mystery" cults? Their rituals and practices were kept secret, which is why we know so little about their exact beliefs and activities.[2] This was on purpose. Privacy enticed new people and helped worshipers "in the know" to carry a sense of enlightenment and privilege.

The popular mystery cults from the Greco-Roman world that we know the most about often have ancient or foreign roots, or both. Because of the diverse geographic origins of these cults, they had some differences of practice and ideology, but they tend to be lumped together by ancient historians of religion because of some key similarities.

*Secrecy.* First and foremost, they operated as private cults, inviting interested parties into initiation before they could experience the fullness of what the patron deities had to offer, and even then worshipers had to move through tiers to reach further illumination. To maintain a measure of exclusivity and to protect privacy, mystery cults met in unpopulated areas, often at night.

*Initiation and membership.* Those who pursued participation in mystery cults could not simply come and go. The cults

## Greco-Roman Mystery Cults

| Name | Origins | Gods | Distinctives |
|---|---|---|---|
| Eleusinian Mysteries | Eleusis, Greece | Demeter and Persephone | Influenced by Homeric *Hymn to Demeter*. |
| Samothracian Mysteries | Samothrace, Greece | The Kabeiroi (corresponding to Demeter, Persephone, Hades, Hermes) | As Samothrace was an island, pilgrimage to honor the great gods in their sanctuary there brought special blessing to seafarers. |
| Bacchic/ Dionysiac Mysteries | Ancient Greece | Bacchus/ Dionysius | Known to perform their secret rituals in the wilderness (often in caves) and to use alcohol and drugs to facilitate "transcendence." |
| Isis Mysteries | Egypt | Isis (Egyptian goddess) | Isis was an all-powerful mother goddess and promised devotees salvation in the afterlife. |
| Cult of Mithras | India and/or Iran | Mithras (Indo-Iranian sun god) | Roman Mithraism had sophisticated levels of progression: initiates began in the level of Raven and moved through the ranks of Bridegroom, Soldier, Lion, Persian, Sun-Carrier, and Father. |

required serious commitment, not only to certain gods but to a community as well. The process of initiation and official membership was often rigorous, formal, and complex. But the cult was a special community and offered intimacy, comradery, and a powerful shared ecstatic experience. Taking the cult of Isis as an example, George Heyman explains, "Secrecy, coupled with a deep sense of personal commitment and the formation of a new family among those who were true believers, made the cult of Isis a formidable part of ancient Roman religion."[3]

*Myth and liturgy.* Many mystery cults were tied to ancient legends and myths about the history and activities of the patron gods. The cult's liturgy would repeat or refer to those myths.

*Transformation through communion.* Why did men and women go through the rigor and hoops of initiation into these mystery cults? There was a promise of communion or intimacy with a great deity and of blessing and transformation through that numinous contact. Whereas in the state cult contact with the divine was considered volatile and dangerous and could only be mediated through priests, in these private cults the gods were beckoning worshipers to come closer. That was no doubt a major attraction. Communion with the god was often achieved through ecstatic modes induced by high-sensory experiences via drugs, alcohol, sex, and blood sacrifice. And, in contrast to the state cult, these mystery-cult gods offered the promise of abundant blessing in the afterlife.

*For "everyone," if you can pay.* Many of the popular mystery cults leveled the social world of worshipers by accepting slaves and women as having equal status (before the patron gods) as the free men involved. This would have been a major draw for marginalized people. The state cult privileged high-class men, who were often invited to become priests of prestigious temples or who had positions of honor in the many religious festivals. But mystery cults appeared to welcome everyone

Yann Forget/from Le Musée absolu, Phaidon, 10-2C12/Wikimedia Commons/public domain

**Figure 10.1.** Wall fresco in Pompeii at the Villa of the Mysteries. Scholars believe this depicts initiation into a Bacchic mystery cult. While a satyr plays the pipes and a nymph feeds a goat, the initiate (far right) is in a frenzy. On the left side two women appear to be preparing a liquid ritual; playing the lyre is Silenus, commonly known as a drinking companion of the god Bacchus.

equally but typically had a fee for membership that did present a barrier and separated the haves from the have-nots.

Rome tolerated these mystery religions. The state saw a benefit in honoring many gods—the more the better if they brought blessings to Rome and its people. But Rome also kept an eye on these cults, because they could lead to shameful behavior and inappropriate commingling with the divine.[4] The historian Livy recounts how two Roman consuls had to divert their attention away from war efforts to address inappropriate cult behavior.[5]

Livy reports that a suspicious Greek entered Etruria (modern-day Tuscany) and brought "secret nocturnal mysteries."[6] It would have been of little concern to Roman authorities, except that a cult developed and grew rapidly. Reportedly, these worshipers, young and old, got drunk and engaged in orgies, forsaking any sense of modesty and allowing all manner of debauchery.[7] There were also reports of the gatherings indicating that they involved false testimonies, false documents, poisonings, even murder. And the cries of the victims could not even be heard over the beating of ritual drums and cymbals. Livy describes this as a kind of pestilence that swept across the land, even making its way to Rome. Livy also recounts how some cults would force initiates to defile themselves sexually or be killed in sacrifice: "To regard nothing as impious or criminal was the very sum of their religion."[8] In his account, these mysteries suffered from frenzy and hysteria, men running around with madness, moving their bodies in a wild manner, their hair disheveled. Those who refused to participate in certain rituals might be tied up and dumped in a dark cave. With a significant dose of exaggeration for effect, Livy exclaims, "They formed an immense multitude, almost equal to the population of Rome."[9] The consuls conducted interviews of participants and made a report to the Senate, which swiftly outlawed these cults and made involvement illegal.

This story showcases the nature of mystery cults in the Roman world: popular among the masses because of the thrill of the experience and the chance to touch a part of the celestial being—and a good reason to party and make a mess. Rome tolerated these gatherings as long as they did not get out of hand. The problem was, they sometimes got out of hand.

## Was Early Christianity Another Mystery Cult?

We have already seen that critics of the early Christians made accusations against them similar to those Livy leveled against a Greek mystery cult jeopardizing Roman life and civilized piety in his time. Christians were also accused of secrecy since they met in houses in the early morning or at night. They too venerated a foreign god. They sang hymns to their ancient patron deity (Phil. 2:6–11; Col. 1:15–20). They drank wine in a regular religious ritual. They had initiation rites with water. The worshipers were not required to purchase a membership, but they did give money—sometimes all their money (Acts 4:32–35). They practiced ritual "kissing" (the holy kiss of peace; see 1 Pet. 5:14). They claimed to be filled with the divine Spirit and engaged in magic (e.g., healings) and divination (prophecy; see 1 Cor. 12:4–11). They promised salvation, redemption, and heavenly reward (Col. 1:9–14). With these ingredients, one could see how rumors might spread that these Jesus cults were another mystery group, rising in popularity especially among common folk.[10] Remember when Peter had to explain to the crowd at Pentecost that they were not drunk but filled with God's Spirit (Acts 2:15)? Imagine churches having to explain that over and over again throughout the empire.

Anyone who spent any amount of time with the kinds of Christian communities we see in the New Testament would immediately observe key differences with the mystery cults. First of all, while the Christians valued privacy, they did not dwell on secrets; they proclaimed a mystery revealed, but no one had to go through initiation rites to acquire this knowledge.[11] Furthermore, Christians emphasized sobriety and sexual purity (1 Thess. 4:3–4), which they considered a natural outworking of the holy standards of the Jewish covenant. In the mystery cults, one often grew closer to the divine through giving in to overwhelming desires, like sex and drunkenness. Christians believed they were called to the opposite.

Besides this, you know what time it is, how it is now the moment for you to wake from sleep. For salvation is nearer to us now than when we became believers; the night is far gone, the day is near. Let us then lay aside the works of darkness and put on the armor of light; let us live honorably as in the day, not in reveling and drunkenness, not in debauchery and licentiousness, not in quarreling and jealousy. Instead, put on the Lord Jesus Christ, and make no provision for the flesh, to gratify its desires. (Rom. 13:11–14)

It's impossible to say for sure, but it might be that Paul here is calling out the mystery cults in Rome for engaging in precisely this kind of debauchery. Christians made a sharp distinction between the delirium caused by wine and the pure euphoria of being filled with the Holy Spirit (Eph. 5:18). And

## The Cult of Isis and Salvation by Faith

In the ancient Greek novel *Metamorphoses* by Apuleius, we learn about a man named Lucius who is accidentally transformed into a donkey. He receives aid from the Egyptian goddess Isis to help him become human again. The language used of Isis's beneficence has a lot of parallels with Christian imagery and symbolism. In book 11 of *Metamorphoses*, the donkey-form Lucius goes to the sea, plunges himself seven times in the water for purification, and prays to Isis, the great goddess.[a] Lucius calls her "Queen of Heaven" and pleads on her mercy for help. In an instant, he receives a revelation of Isis. She calls out to him, "Behold, Lucius, here I am moved by your prayer, I, mother of all Nature and mistress of the elements, first-born of the ages [cf. Col. 1:15] and greatest powers divine, queen of the dead, and queen of the immortals, all gods and goddesses in a single form" (*Metamorphoses* 11.5). She promises to Lucius friendship and aid: "Weep no more, end your lamentations. Banish sorrow. With my aid, your day of salvation [cf. 2 Cor. 6:2] is at hand" (11.5). She claims to be able to stop blizzards and calm the ocean's storms (sound familiar? see Mark 4:38–40). She invites Lucius to have true faith in her so that she can effect this miracle to restore his form (Matt. 9:22). "Remember one thing clearly though, and keep it locked deep within your heart: the life that is left to you, to the final sigh of yet if an apostle was talking to Bacchanalians (worshipers of Bacchus) or Isisians (worshipers of Isis), they might find common interest in desiring to see the glory of God and becoming transformed more and more into the divine likeness through the Spirit (2 Cor. 3:18).

## *Imitatio Dei*: Modeling the Morality of the Divine

Joining mystery cults was one way of trying to be like the gods, seeking out a mystical heavenly experience. These were

your last breath, is pledged to me" (11.6). If Lucius stays faithful, he will have eternal bliss and honor, and after death he will be with Isis in the Elysian fields, worshiping her for eternity (cf. Luke 23:43). Through his obedience and pure devotion, "I alone can extend your life beyond the limits set by fate" (11.6; cf. John 6:47).

Long story short, she sends him to a festival of her mystery cult, a procession in honor of "the Goddess who saves" (*Metamorphoses* 11.8; cf. Ps. 68:20). He encounters the great priest of Isis and receives a blessing: "At last [you reached] the Harbor of Peace, the altar of Mercy" (11.15). The priest calls Lucius to find his place as a believer in "this holy cadre," to dedicate himself to this cult, to submit his will, and to know true freedom through service to the mother goddess Isis (11.15).

Lucius recounts to the reader the preparations for official initiation into the cult of Isis but stops short of describing the initiation itself for the reader: "I'd tell you, if it were allowed" (*Metamorphoses* 11.23). All that he is able to share is that he descended to the gates of death and came back to a new illumination. He experienced the true presence of the gods below and above and gave them proper worship. After he was inducted into the cult as a new member, he wept, washing the goddess statue's feet with his tears, and prayed to the "holy and eternal savior of humankind" (11.24; cf. Jude 25).

a. Quotations are from Apuleius, *The Golden Ass*, trans., notes, and preface by P. G. Walsh (Oxford: Oxford University Press, 1999), 218–21.

popular but not everyone's cup of tea. Another approach to becoming divine-like was through imitation. For this we turn to the Greco-Roman moral philosophers, who mostly dismissed ecstatic forms of worship and instead promoted the virtues of learning the higher moral ways of the gods.

Now, your average Roman on the street did not think very highly of the morality of the Olympians. The Olympians had power and status, but they had the same moral flaws as humans: they bickered and were jealous, vengeful, conniving, and petty. Read Homer. Read Virgil. You honored the gods because they were powerful, not noble.

But the Stoic philosophers thought of the gods differently. Some gods were bad models—that's undeniable—but the best of the gods were great teachers, the ideals for forming a proper lifestyle. For example, Epictetus, citing the Greek philosopher Zeno, claimed that it was humankind's true end to imitate the ways of the gods.[12] And a true Stoic was one who "has set his heart upon changing from a man into a god, and although he is still in this paltry body of death, does none the less have his purpose set upon fellowship with Zeus."[13] This was the way to become godlike, not by indulging in wine and drugs in pursuit of transcendence but by adopting the mindset, virtues, and behaviors of the gods: "If the deity is faithful, [the worshiper] must be faithful. . . . If high-minded, he also must be high-minded, and so forth; therefore, in everything he says and does, he must act as an imitator of God."[14]

Seneca wrote similarly about living like the gods. He acknowledged that humans could never be as great and perfect as the gods, but people were to imitate them as closely as possible, to approach them morally, even if they would never arrive.[15] What exactly was meant to be imitated? Seneca mentioned "reason," interpreting and responding to a situation as is good and right.[16] Fellow Stoic Musonius Rufus was once asked for his advice about how to live to a happy old age. He responded by saying that young and old both ought to live according to nature and virtue, not pleasure and power. Musonius went on to say that mortals were meant to resemble the gods who were impervious to and unconquered by desire, greed, envy, and jealousy. On the contrary, they were magnanimous, gracious, and kind; insofar as mortals were shaped in that image, they must conform to those virtues and the classic morals of prudence, justice, courage, and temperance.[17]

## Imitators of Christ

In several places the New Testament encourages imitation of God, along similar lines as we have seen in the Greco-Roman Stoics.

> Therefore be imitators of God. (Eph. 5:1)

> And you became imitators . . . of the Lord. (1 Thess. 1:6)

> God is love, and those who abide in love abide in God, and God abides in them. (1 John 4:16)

> Do not imitate what is evil but imitate what is good. Whoever does good is from God; whoever does evil has not seen God. (3 John 11)

But the Christian tradition goes much deeper in its emphasis on imitating and conforming to the ways of God. While this idea is occasionally present among the Stoics, these philosophers were more focused on accepting fate than on transforming into the moral nature of God. For Christians, growing into the likeness of God was a priority, and Jesus Christ was the pattern or blueprint. We will look at several concepts that explain or express this.

*You become what you worship.*[18] The first concept is embedded in Jewish thought and inscribed into the Old Testament and early Jewish literature. The idea is this: a worshiper will naturally conform to the likeness and features of what is worshiped. Psalm 115 captures this well. The psalmist explains why Israel does not have idols of their gods. God lives in the heavens; he is not at the beck and call of mortals. The nations have their idols and think that their gods are present with them, but these simpleminded idol worshipers don't understand that they are doomed to become just like their false gods of wood and metal and stone.

> They have mouths, but do not speak;
>   eyes, but do not see.
> They have ears, but do not hear;
>   noses, but do not smell.
> They have hands, but do not feel;
>   feet, but do not walk;
>   they make no sound in their throats.
> Those who make them are like them;
>   so are all who trust in them. (115:5–8)

So idol worshipers will become just like their venerated statues: blind, dumb, and lifeless. The alternative is to worship the one true and living God and imitate his manner and character. Throughout the Old Testament, we find the language of living like YHWH, literally "walking in his ways." Israel is commanded to keep the laws of God, "by walking in his ways and fearing him" (Deut. 8:6). Prosperity is promised for Israel as they love God, observe his decrees, and walk in his ways (30:16). Another psalmist sums up the blessed life:

> Happy is everyone who fears the LORD
>   who walks in his ways.

You shall eat the fruit of the labor of your hands;
you shall be happy, and it shall go well with you.
(Ps. 128:1–2)

The New Testament draws from this idea that worshipers become just like their gods. There is a natural bending or conformity toward the deity. One way that the New Testament writers express this is in terms of a particular pattern or "image." Adam, of course, was created in the image of God, and thus he was the mold for humanity going forward. But when Adam sinned, that once-pristine image became deformed, which then corrupted all who were born into Adam's form. Imagine an ink stamp containing a flaw. Every time that stamp is used, the imprint will be wrong. That's the kind of idea that is found in the New Testament. Jesus Christ, then, became a new and perfect image that could reshape this corrupt humanity. Paul explains to the Corinthians, "Just as we have borne the image of the man of dust [Adam], we will also bear the image of the man of heaven [Jesus]" (1 Cor. 15:49). Paul describes this elsewhere as a gradual process of transformation, the Holy Spirit performing a kind of spiritual laser surgery to shape the believer into the likeness of the Son of God (Rom. 8:29; 2 Cor. 3:18; Col. 3:10). This transformation into the likeness of Christ has a natural moral effect: those who clothe themselves with Christ conform to Christ's own behavior. Colossians, especially, emphasizes imitating Christ's compassion, kindness, humility, meekness, and patience (Col. 3:12).

*Children become like parents.* Another way the New Testament gets at this idea of imitation is the ancient notion that children grow up to be like their parents. We know this is true physically. There are family resemblances in height, frame, hair color, and other features. But this was also believed to be true in terms of habits, attitudes, and morality. The author of the Jewish text 4 Maccabees explains that parents "impress upon the character of a small child a wondrous likeness both of mind and of form" (15:4). He goes on to explain how the children of a good mother will conform to her nobility, love, and piety (15:5–10).[19] In the record of the teachings of Jesus, this can be seen in his aphorism "Be perfect, therefore, as your heavenly Father is perfect" (Matt. 5:48). This is not a teacher's harsh demand for absolutely excellent, flawless behavior. Rather, this is a loving parent's invitation to grow in maturity as the parent is mature.[20] Paul refers to God as the "Father of mercies . . . and consolation" (2 Cor. 1:3), encouraging human mercy to one another. James writes about the "Father of lights" who is gracious and reliable (James 1:17). Given the invisible and transcendent nature of the heavenly Father, it would have been somewhat hard for believers to conceive of how to imitate such a grand and mysterious being. More often, the early Christians pointed to imitating the Son of God, Jesus. Within this "family" conception, Jesus would be like the oldest brother, who is a model for the younger siblings (Phil. 2:5–11).

*The Christian life produces fruit.* Similar to this conception of familial conformity is the early Christian emphasis on moral and spiritual fruit production. The Christian life is conceived of as a progressive movement toward blossoming and ripe fruitfulness. In Matthew, Jesus talks about knowing the truth about a person by looking at the "fruit" of their lives (Matt. 7:16; 12:33; 21:43). In John, we find a more comprehensive image of Jesus as the great vine and the disciples as living branches who find their vitality in him. The branches, by their nature, are to be nourished by the vine and bear healthy fruit (John 15:5–11). So Jesus commands his disciples, "Go and bear fruit, fruit that will last" (15:16).

The apostolic writers continued to use these images of organic flourishing and fecundity. Paul exhorts believers to "bear fruit for God" (Rom. 7:4; cf. Col. 1:10); walk in step with the Spirit and experience the Spirit's fruit of love, joy, peace, and so forth (Gal. 5:22–23); and grow together as one healthy communal body with Christ as the living "head" (Eph. 4:15; Col. 2:19). In a similar vein Peter speaks of living a thriving Christian life by longing for nutrition that enables growth toward God's good end (1 Pet. 2:2).

It is difficult for modern readers of the Bible to grasp how out of place "fruitfulness" language would be in view of traditional Roman religion. State religion was not concerned with personal formation, maturity, or fruitfulness. The goal was to placate the gods and secure their blessing. The gods didn't care much about human maturity, certainly not on an individual level. As long as mortals paid their respects, made their sacrifices, and honored the celestial beings, all would be fine.

## Becoming Like Christ

Now, those who sought out the mystery cults wanted something more experiential and soul touching. And often the mystery cults promised stages of transcendence and deeper knowledge of the patron gods. But this progression through stages had little to do with morality and virtue for most participants.[21] It was about unlocking mysteries and mystical experiences through ritual and allegiance. The moral philosophers, especially the Stoics, wanted moral formation but didn't much refer to intimacy. The gods were models and teachers, not family and friends. These weird Christians seemed to have combined the existential desires of the mysteries and the pedagogical aspirations of the philosophers. But the Christians were not trying to piece together a new religion from these fragments of Roman society. Their religious pursuits derived from the Jewish covenantal conception of a formative relationship with God, which was reshaped by uniting with the Messiah, Jesus, and a unique transformation by God's singular Spirit.

177

Christians pursued a lifestyle of pleasing God and becoming Godlike, not for the sake of power or status but to become truly human, made in God's image and remade into the likeness of Christ. That meant imitating Christ's character, his humility, love, righteousness, and purity.

# To Treat All as Equal

For in Christ Jesus you are all children of God through faith.
As many of you as were baptized into Christ have clothed
yourselves with Christ. There is no longer Jew or Greek,
there is no longer slave or free, there is no longer male and
female; for all of you are one in Christ Jesus.

St. Paul, Galatians 3:26–28

From the beginning of this book, I have emphasized that
for most ancient religions—including Roman religion—
the veneration of the gods was not a hobby or a private
matter. It was woven into the fabric of personal and corporate
life, and in many ways it was the most important matter. Con-
sequently, it was inevitable that a person's values and lifestyle
would be shaped by what they think about the gods and by
what the gods think about mortals. If religion was *everything*,
then everything would be shaped by the will and the ways
of the gods. If the gods didn't care about mortals, then that
would reflect on the value of humanity. We have also seen that

179

worshipers naturally emulate their gods (and, ironically, they end up creating gods in their own image). The bottom line is this: the behavior of the gods becomes the behavior of the humans; they are teachers and "lifestyle influencers," whether they want to be or not.

When we look at the lifestyles of the Greek and Roman gods, especially according to sacred myths and legends, we find a mix of good and bad, virtues and vices, not unlike the realm of mortals. Gods could be noble, altruistic, and gracious. They could also be conniving, vengeful, and sinister. Some remained pure; others sought pleasure. Some cultivated peace; others brought war and violence. But the broader pattern we see in the "culture" of the gods is one of power-seeking and domination. In chapter 4 we briefly looked at the *Theogony*, Hesiod's account of the generations of the gods. This celestial history is far from a tale of gracious cooperation in a cosmic utopia. Uranus (the sky god) hates his own children and hides them away; Gaia enables them to take revenge, led by Cronus. Cronus sits in power, but ironically his own child is prophesied to overthrow him. And that child, Zeus, starts the *Titanomachy*, the war of the gods and titans. When Zeus emerges victorious, he is hailed as the supreme deity, but we know from many Greek legends that he has ongoing conflicts with his fellow Olympians. The world of the gods is survival of the fittest, and those in power always have targets on their backs. There is a clear hierarchy. You know where you sit in the pyramid of power, and you try to prevent people on the lower end from coming up while trying to move higher yourself.

How could it not be the same for mortals? The Roman world on earth was designed to reflect the inherent power structure of the gods. "Might makes right," as the saying goes. There was class, there was strength, there were those who deserved greatness, and there were those who didn't. There was nobility, and there was commonness. There were kings, and there were slaves. As in heaven, so on earth. Everyone watched what was going on up above, where the action was. When Roman children asked for a bedtime story, they wanted to hear of war victories of the gods and great Olympian contests of power.

What is interesting to me is how the Christians talked about God. Their stories are different. Yes, God is great, supreme, unmatched in wisdom and strength. But the legends they learned and sang in worship were about the *humility* of God. In Philippians 2:5–11, we catch a glimpse of how Christians sang odes to their patron deity, Jesus Christ.

> Let the same mind be in you that was in Christ Jesus,
>> who, though he was in the form of God,
>>> did not regard equality with God
>>> as something to be exploited,
>> but emptied himself,
>>> taking the form of a slave,
>>> being born in human likeness.
>> And being found in human form,
>>> he humbled himself
>>> and became obedient to the point of death—
>>> even death on a cross.
>
> Therefore God also highly exalted him
>> and gave him the name
>> that is above every name,
> so that at the name of Jesus
>> every knee should bend,
>> in heaven and on earth and under the earth,
> and every tongue should confess
>> that Jesus Christ is Lord,
>> to the glory of God the Father.

What a strange ode! Most people dreamed of ascent, climbing up the ladder of power and success. Even gods craved more power and status. But here is this supreme deity who intentionally climbs down. And not only does he descend into the mortal realm but he becomes *human*, and not just in appearance but *actually* human. And even more than that, he takes a lowly form, not like that of a king or warrior but like that of a slave, a nobody. And there's more! He dies. (That's odd.) But there's even more—he dies the very worst kind of death. Death on a cross, a traitor's death, a slave's death, a death with no honor or dignity. It was Rome's way of rendering someone insignificant. What powerful being would allow such a thing to happen to them? But there's more to the story. God the Father raises this Son Jesus up from the grave and honors him with even higher status. Why? Because what he did, he did out of love for humanity and obedience to the Father. Here is a truly selfless being, and the focus is not on his physical powers (though he had those) but on his *love*. And notice how Paul begins: "You mortals, adopt this same mindset. Be just like this supreme being, not in aspirations of greatness, but in humility, service, obedience, and love."

## The Gods Have Come Down to Us in Human Form!

Greek and Roman myths and novels are filled with stories of gods coming down to earth in human form for one reason or another. Homer's *Odyssey* depicts the goddess Athena disguising herself as Mentes, Telemachus's old friend, to give him counsel. Zeus was especially known to mask his true identity while on earth. In Plautus's *Amphitryon*, discussed in chapter 1, he disguises himself as the husband of the human woman Alcmene so that he can sleep with her. His trick works, and Alcmene becomes pregnant with Heracles (Hercules is the Roman equivalent of Heracles). But Zeus wasn't always this underhanded when he took on the appearance of a mortal.

**Figure 11.1.** Jupiter and Mercury received by Philemon and Baucis, by Adolphe Déchenaud (1891)

In another famous story, from Ovid's *Metamorphoses*, Zeus and Hermes walk the earth incognito as peasant travelers. Looking for a place to stay, they are turned away by wealthy folks who can certainly afford to help these wayfarers. A poor Phrygian couple named Philemon and Baucis welcome these two strangers in and give them food, the best they can provide with their meager provisions (see fig. 11.1). As a reward for their gracious and generous hospitality, Zeus and Hermes warn them of a coming flood and lead them to safety. Greeks sometimes called him "Zeus Xenios," protector of strangers and guardian of inns. This reflects a Greek tradition of *theoxenia* ("giving hospitality to the gods"). Pamela Johnston aptly explains the cultural value of this story for ancient Greeks: "One should always offer hospitality to strangers on the possibility that the prospective guest might be a god in disguise."[1] Stories like these were a salutary sign that the gods cared about

183

what was happening on earth. They genuinely wanted humans to imitate certain virtues, in this case care for strangers.

We find a somewhat similar scenario in the Gospel of Luke, where Jesus, after his death and resurrection, appears to two disciples walking on the road to the village of Emmaus. As Jesus converses with them, "their eyes were kept from recognizing him" (Luke 24:16). Playing dumb, Jesus asks them about the commotion they are discussing. Only after they explain that their teacher, Jesus, is dead and gone does Jesus break character, so to speak, and call them out on their lack of faith and insight. Jesus teaches them the proper way to view what God is doing as they make their way to Emmaus. Once they arrive, Jesus indicates he is going to part ways with them, but they invite him to stay with them (there's that hospitality again!). He accepts, and when he breaks bread and gives it to them, *then* their eyes are opened. Jesus then vanishes (24:31). This experience prompts the two disciples to return to Jerusalem immediately and proclaim the resurrection. There are some interesting parallels with Zeus and Hermes, but here is the big difference: Jesus is never *pretending* to be human. He never wears skin as a disguise. He actually *became* human, and he remains human without losing his godness. He has taken on a hybrid identity, fully god and fully human, something the world had never heard of or seen before. And he did this not as a test, not as part of an experiment, but to rescue sinners, to show compassion on the ungodly, to try to make friends out of enemies.

I want to go back to Paul's reference to Jesus coming in the form of a slave (Phil. 2:7). This isn't about the technical legal status of Jesus; he wasn't actually a slave. I take this more to be a statement about Jesus's humility and attitude toward others. From a cultural perspective, a slave is at the very bottom of society, alongside criminals and immigrants. So, to put it bluntly, slaves are never in a position to look down on anyone. Calling Jesus a slave is a reminder of his disregard for human estimations of status, privilege, and power. The Roman world was set up and thrived on a clear index of power based on demographics like location, ethnicity, citizenship, gender, legal status, and occupation. A typical Roman would evaluate a person according to these factors, but Jesus modeled and taught a radically subversive sociology. Jesus had honest and vulnerable conversations with women. Jesus encouraged fellow Jews to admire virtuous Samaritans, whom many Jews saw as enemies. Jesus valued children in a society that saw them only as *future* contributors.

In terms of Jesus's status-toppling ethic, one story stands out to me. In Matthew 20, we have the awkward situation where the mother of the sons of Zebedee asks Jesus to make her children the two greatest in his kingdom. (Talk about a major mom-embarrassment moment; I've been there.) Jesus takes this opportunity to teach the Twelve about the way of the kingdom. "You know that the rulers of the Gentiles [like Caesar] lord it over them, and their great ones are tyrants over them. It will not be so among you; but whoever wishes to be great among you must be your servant, and whoever wishes to be first among you must be your slave; just as the Son of Man came not to be served but to serve, and to give his life a ransom for many" (Matt. 20:25–28).

This is quite the upending teaching. The *first* will be a *slave?* This simply wouldn't compute with a Romanized way of structuring society. Romans had class and nobility on the one side and commoners and slaves on the other side. Jesus was blurring these lines, eliminating privilege and calling the highest and greatest to service.

To illustrate how this is quite different from a traditional Roman perspective, I want to point to a letter from Pliny the Younger to Tiro (a.k.a. Titus Calestrius Tiro Orbius Speratus, Roman praetor). Pliny is writing to his colleague to encourage him. He even exhorts Tiro to act with generosity and kindness in his position. Pliny reminds him to act with fairness and even graciousness to all, whether to those below him or to those above. But Pliny also reminds him: there is a temptation to gain the favor of your inferiors by talking bad about your superiors. Pliny warns Tiro not to cozy up to his inferiors in this way, blurring the lines of class and rank. Then Pliny makes an infamous claim: "Nothing can be more unequal than the appearance of equality which is thus produced."[2] What Pliny means is that promoting this false equality by chumming up to your inferiors will only make things worse and will actually threaten the order of Roman social existence. Romans prized cooperation, not equality. There could be fairness, justice, and even mercy on occasion, but equality would only lead to chaos. Olympus wasn't flat, and neither will Rome be.

This chapter is all about how the way of the gods shapes the way of mortals. Pliny was no doubt affected by his theology and "theonomy"—how a certain social order is maintained by heaven. The Roman way proclaimed justice (*iustitia*) and peace (*pax*), but these were meant to be interpreted from a distinctly Roman perspective, which reinforced class and status. All could have "bread and circuses" (popular entertainment),* but only some deserved mansions and healthcare.

Jesus and the early Christians taught something different: each person is made in the image of God, God does not pay attention to status, he has no favorites, all will face judgment, and all have equal access to divine grace and mercy.

## The Social Fiction of Saturnalia

In chapter 7 we noted that Romans celebrated a number of religious holidays, many of them focusing on one deity or

---

*This famous line comes from the Roman satire writer Juvenal (*Satires* 10.80–81) and refers to how the emperor would try to pacify the subjugated masses by giving them cheap entertainment and food.

an event of divine intervention. Saturnalia, a winter festival honoring the god Saturn, was the most popular event. Roman historian Jerry Toner paints a vivid picture of the goings-on of Saturnalia. Romans viewed the ancient golden age of Saturn as a time of equality and prosperity. There was no social class, no slavery, no wealth gap. All of life and human resources were shared in common, a utopian socialism—in the form of a big party. The Roman celebrations of Saturnalia may remind us of the reckless jubilation of Mardi Gras, with its dirty songs and wild and erotic dancing, things that could get you arrested the very next day for "disorderly conduct."[3] Sometimes partying is just partying, but on the surface of things, there seems to have been a point to all of this—everyone got to share in pleasure and abundance, not just the rich. "The whole world is turned upside down," Toner explains.[4] Anything goes. Commoners could tease anyone and not get in trouble. They could mouth off at princes and governors, insult the emperor, and even taunt the gods. For just one festival, a small slice of the year, everyone lived in a bizzarro world where slaves wore the fancy clothes of the elite, and elites tried on the rags of the poor. The least among society got a taste of the Roman dream. But Toner makes a sober point: at the end of the festival, it proved to be just that, a sweet dream that quickly dissipated into the waking reality and drudgery of their real Roman life. Toner uses historical fiction to voice the perspective of a wealthy, elite Roman man reflecting on the jocularity of Saturnalia, which adds up to nothing of substance.

> I think they are simply fun holidays, mere opportunities for the people to let off a bit of steam without really changing anything. In fact, they serve to emphasise how we [elites] expect the norms of behaviour to be observed throughout the rest of the year. . . . The Saturnalia reinforces the social hierarchy by underlining what a temporary period of transgression and

relief this is. . . . It is a release of the tensions that build up in normal life. Society works better as a result, if only we have seen how ridiculous and chaotic the world would be if we did not have normal rules. . . . The Saturnalia teaches all of us, slaves above all, how stupid and impossible it would be to change the existing order of things because the result would be a foolish mess.[5]

Let me reiterate a few things here. Of all the events of the Roman calendar year, this was the blowout festival, the craziest week of partying you can imagine.[6] Latin poet Catullus called it the "best of days."[7] This was Fourth of July, Christmas, Thanksgiving, and Halloween all wrapped into one. There was alcohol aplenty, along with games, gambling, dancing, theater, music, and presents. Children were allowed to break free from social expectations of silence and decorum and run wild.[8] As you can imagine, there was a lot of noise and fanfare, which reminds me of the subversion of Guy Fawkes Day in England. Pliny the Younger found it all so bothersome that he would immediately isolate himself in his private study to get away from the din and nonsense.[9]

From Toner's description above, you can see that the festival tried to replicate a kind of ancient golden age under Saturn where men were equal (women didn't much factor into this holiday, except as "entertainers"). Slaves, in particular, were given an opportunity to live like free men and even boss around their bosses.[10] Masters might serve dinner to their own slaves.[11] Not everyone would dare to go that far, but there were reports that the emperor Lucius Verus allowed some of his slaves to dine at his own table, a thought that was unfathomable any other week of the year.[12] (As the old Roman saying goes, the more slaves you have, the more enemies you have.)[13]

Lucian of Samosata explained that the point of it all was to allow a slave to feel like a king for just one moment; but everyone knew, in the end, it was all still a fiction, a bunch of silliness and nonsense.[14] It's like opposite day, a chance to be immature but not a real world at all. Classics scholar Fanny Dolansky explains that this social inversion during Saturnalia was probably, from the perspective of Roman elites, less about honoring and rewarding slaves and more about giving them something to look forward to once a year to prevent revolts and runaways: "For masters, extending these temporary privileges was considered preventive—essential for diffusing tensions engendered by the servile condition that threatened the welfare of the entire household."[15] Saturnalia was fun, but ultimately that was all it was for the least and the last. Putting the last first (which might resemble Christian values on the surface) was seemingly applied for a short while in the middle of December, but for the rest of the year, the last were still very much last.

## To Treat All as Equal

There is a line repeated throughout early Christian literature: with God, there are no favorite people. God doesn't prefer one ethnicity (Rom. 2:11). God doesn't prefer masters over slaves (Eph. 6:9; Col. 3:25).[16] This is picked up and fleshed out in the letter of James in relation to how mortals ought to treat one another as believers-in-Jesus: "My brothers and sisters, do you with your acts of favoritism really believe in our glorious Lord Jesus Christ?" (James 2:1). James goes on to illustrate how rich and poor in the assembly should be treated the same (2:2–7). There is no "first class" in the church. Because Christ is blind to privilege, believers must be as well. Favoritism cannot exist where people obey the commandment "You shall love your neighbor as yourself" (2:8). Now, this matter is brought up in James probably because believers were not always treating everyone equally. This was an aspiration, not a full reality.

But we do see that this value was reinforced throughout early Christian teaching.

A more explicit Christian statement of status-leveling equality is found in Paul's letter to the Galatians: "As many of you as were baptized into Christ have clothed yourselves with Christ. There is no longer Jew or Greek, there is no longer slave or free, there is no longer male and female; for all of you are one in Christ Jesus" (3:27–28). This theological declaration comes in the midst of Paul's argument that Gentiles (non-Jews) are welcomed into the family of the one God *as* Gentiles and on equal footing as Jews. Jews have long been God's special and holy people, a "treasured possession" (Exod. 19:5). Paul, a Jew, is not denying that (see Rom. 9:4). But the coming of the Messiah means that there will be a blessing not only for Jews— Jews first and foremost, in fact (Rom. 1:16–17)—but also for Gentiles, because this one great Lord Jesus will welcome any and all into his kingdom, regardless of background, birth, or status (Col. 1:13–14).

In his letter to the Galatians, Paul argues that anyone who identifies with Jesus Christ (and is united with him through the Spirit) is seen by God not according to ethnicity but only according to their relationship to Christ. In 3:27–28, Paul reinforces his point by drawing from what is probably early Christian liturgy, perhaps even liturgy related to the baptism ceremony. To be baptized into Christ is to leave behind old ways of looking at humanity; believers are washed, cleaned, and made holy (1 Cor. 6:11). To be clothed with Christ (Gal. 3:27) is for *all* to be given Christ's own stamp of acceptance and belonging. Galatians 3:28 might have been some kind of confession that was made during initiation, reminding these new Jesus people that they would not be compared to each other based on demographics and worldly estimations of importance and worth.

To say "there is no longer Jew or Greek" did not mean that ethnicity would vanish. It simply meant that ethnicity would not be a dividing line of favor and power in the kingdom of God. Paul does not dismiss slavery as an institution, as much as we wish he would have. But to claim that "there is no longer slave or free" means that slaves should be treated with the same dignity and respect as the free. And "no longer male and female" means that negative stereotypes should not be forced onto women. All become identified with Christ. All receive the same honor and respect that one would afford to the Lord himself. If this text is some kind of early confession, that means equality was a cornerstone belief among the early Christians. If God does not play favorites, how can we (Acts 10:34)?

It's one thing for Paul to write this out as an aspiration, but was it an actual practice? Is there evidence that Christians actually broke with status expectations of Roman society? Put another way, would Pliny (who warned Tiro about equality) have seen Paul's churches as weird or, worse, dangerous? I think we do have evidence along these lines. I want to turn to a place that may not seem relevant on first glance but that happens to be a goldmine of information about early Christianity: the greetings at the end of Paul's letter to the Romans (16:1–16). Paul recognizes numerous Christians in Rome: Prisca and Aquila (and their house church), Epaenetus, Mary, Andronicus and Junia, Ampliatus, Urbanus, Stachys, Apelles, the family of Aristobulus, Herodion, the family of Narcissus, Tryphaena and Tryphosa, Persis, Rufus and his mother, Asyncritus, Phlegon, Hermes, Patrobas, Hermas, Philologus, Julia, Nereus and his sister, and Olympas. That's almost thirty individuals, and what would have been remarkable and immediately noticeable about this list to the first Roman readers were the sheer diversity of these people *and* that they were not listed according to worldly status.

In a traditional Romanized list of people, it would be conventional to list the high-status people first (like you would today when thanking donors at a charity event). In the list

191

in Romans 16, all the names are jumbled in terms of worldly status. Women are named alongside men. Several women are named without the mention of a husband or father (as with Tryphaena and Tryphosa). Jewish names are mixed together with Latin and Greek names. And perhaps most shocking, slaves are commended alongside free people. Now, we don't know exactly who in this list was a slave; Paul doesn't make that explicit. But scholars have studied the names themselves carefully, and several names in this greeting are typical names of slaves. Often, slaves would be named after a deity, like Hermes, or a very basic attribute. For instance, Ampliatus means "large," and Urbanus means "city person."

We don't know how intentional this list is in terms of Paul showcasing blind appreciation. But it is very noticeable that Paul does not tailor his praise to specific stereotypes. He doesn't commend slaves as obedient, masters as powerful, men as strong, or women as sweet or loyal. In general, for each kind of person he simply says that they work hard for the Lord or that they are beloved by God. Their value is seen in their relationship to the gospel of Jesus Christ. If Romans 16 is a window into early Christianity, then these communities were a jumble of people rubbing shoulders, highborn and not, men and women, slaves and masters, citizens and immigrants. That doesn't mean that everyone got along. In fact, most of the apostolic letters we have in the New Testament were written precisely to remind Christians that they needed to learn how to cooperate and treat each other with grace and love! But the seeds of a whole new sociology and ethos were sown, and we see signs of life in the New Testament.

I want to close this chapter by directing attention to Paul's shortest text, the letter to the Christian slave master Philemon. This is a fascinating window into the real difference that Jesus made, in Paul's mind, for social life together in the midst of real differences. A brief word about the situation: Philemon was a

Christian leader who probably led a house church. We know he had a slave called Onesimus. Onesimus went to see Paul in prison, and through that relationship Onesimus became a believer. In the midst of all of that, there was some kind of estrangement or dispute between Philemon and Onesimus. Many readers of this letter over the years have presumed that Onesimus ran away from his master and Paul sent him home to apologize and make amends. The letter doesn't make that clear. There could be other scenarios, but what Paul wants in the end *is* clear: he is sending Onesimus back home, and Philemon is expected to welcome him with open arms. Now, as you can imagine, that's not how a Roman master would normally treat a slave with whom he had a falling out. Slaves were regularly shamed, abused, beaten, forced into manual labor, or sold into worse circumstances. Slaves were often treated as subhuman, like farm animals or disposable property. Yet Paul calls Philemon to choose a different course of action.

It might be surprising, and disappointing, to consider the fact that Paul does not command or encourage Philemon to set Onesimus free (this was called "manumission"). Apparently, Paul is not especially concerned with a formal change of legal status for Onesimus. Rather, the focus is on how Philemon should *treat* Onesimus: "No longer as a slave but more than a slave, a beloved brother" (Philem. 16). For reasons that we are not entirely sure about, Paul does not generally promote manumission for slaves. What he does want is for masters to treat slaves with respect and dignity and even to treat fellow Christians who are slaves *as family*, brothers and sisters in Christ. That would have been a remarkable statement, because household slaves, while serving a family within the context of a house, were keenly aware that they were not true family. Slaves were not allowed to marry (formally), their own children would immediately become property of the master's family, and they could not own property or even possess their own goods or money. Masters would have little hesitation about satisfying their sexual desires by forcing themselves on their slaves. So for Paul to tell Philemon that Onesimus is really his beloved brother is transformative. But what I think is *really* remarkable is what Paul says next: "Welcome him [home] as you would welcome me" (v. 17). Keep in mind that for many of these churches in the middle of the first century, the apostle Paul was a big deal. He was someone many believers respected and admired, the closest thing to royalty you are going to find, even if Paul didn't want such acclaim (Gal. 2:6). But Paul clearly knew that people saw him as a VIP, and he knew he could use that to get people like Philemon to rethink their social values. What he is communicating is something like this: "Treat this slave of yours, Onesimus, as you would me; welcome him, accept him, show him hospitality, make him your best meal, wash his feet, offer him the best seat to rest from his travels." It feels a bit like the jolly traditions of Saturnalia, except this is real life for Paul. This isn't make-believe. This is how it should be for everyone always, not just during a holiday of silliness.

At the very end of this brief letter, Paul includes a not-so-subtle reminder of his expectations. Paul writes, "One thing more—prepare a guest room for me, for I am hoping through your prayers to be restored to you" (Philem. 22). Notice the wording "prepare a guest room." Paul knows very well what Philemon would do to show hospitality for a VIP. He would roll out the red carpet. This is another reminder that someone like Onesimus should be receiving such gracious hospitality and not just be the one to do all the preparations at the master's bidding.

Today, equality and human rights are values and mottos that are often taken for granted. This was not the case in the ancient world, a time and place with kings, nobility, and slaves acting as foundational elements of society. To treat all as equal would seem, to many, to invite anarchy, like letting children boss around parents. Christians were not the first or only people to promote social equality, but we can see it was built into the DNA of their belief system. They did not always live up to these ideals, but we catch glimpses of that beautiful vision in the New Testament from time to time. Our modern values of equality owe a lot to Greek notions of democracy and the voice of the people, and Roman governance through an organized senate; but the Western notion of the inherent dignity of each individual comes from the Christians, their best teachings and reasonings.

# The Christians
# Were Not Perfect

The name of God is blasphemed among the Gentiles because of you.

St. Paul, Romans 2:24, quoting Isaiah 52:5

Before we get into some concluding reflections in the next chapter, I want to address an important caveat about presenting the early Christians as weird, dangerous, and attractive. The preceding chapters have tried to demonstrate how these Jesus followers deviated from religious and cultural norms of the Roman world of the first century. And in my attempt to underscore the distinctions between Christian religion and Roman religion, it is possible to run the risk of presenting Christians as perfect. This runs parallel to various claims made throughout history about "Christian exceptionalism" or "biblical exceptionalism." This often involves exaggerated claims that a group or ideology is in a class of its own, essentially perfect, and that nothing else could compare. Sometimes I hear about "American exceptionalism," the idea that America is the best country with no near competitors. The reasonable pushback is that these are inflated and self-serving claims. Mindful of that, I want to be careful not to make it appear that Christians were always the glorious exception.

So this short chapter is an opportunity to do a reality check and make it clear that the early Christians were far from perfect. While *in general* I think they were weird, and while I think that they were attractive and compelling in their best moments and as manifestations of Jesus's kingdom vision, the truth is that churches fell short then, just as they do now. Early Christians did not glow with saintly halos. And it is important for the sake of honest history-telling to be reminded of their shortcomings. There are a number of topics I could include here, but I will limit myself to three.

*They fought and competed with one another.* If we just open up the pages of the early Christian writings we find in the New Testament, it quickly becomes clear that unity and generosity toward one another did not come easily. Whether we look at the factionalism in Corinth (1 Cor. 1:10–17), the friction between the "Strong" and the "Weak" in Rome (Rom. 14–15), or the biting and devouring in Galatia (Gal. 5:15), we get the sense that strong opinions meant that rivalry, pride, and malice were all too common in these Jesus assemblies. Even among leaders there was sometimes pretense and trickery (3 John 9).

Paul, for example, confronted Cephas (Peter) in public in Antioch as they had conflict over table fellowship with Gentiles (Gal. 2:11–12). We get the sense that it wasn't unusual for Paul to find himself in disagreement with other leaders over aspects of the gospel, salvation, and the life of the church. In Paul's second letter to the Corinthians, we learn about a rivalry Paul had with a certain group he calls "super-apostles," other leaders who were more impressive to the Corinthians than Paul was (2 Cor. 12:11–13).

There were times when communities fractured and split and warnings were issued—for example, that one group ought to avoid and shun the other. The author of 1 John exhorts his readers to be on the lookout for false prophets who deny the incarnation of Jesus (2:26; 4:2). Those who have left the community are treated with suspicion (2:19). There hardly seems to be a Christian community that we know of from the first century that didn't have problems with unity and cooperation. Perhaps this was inevitable as a new religious cult was forming and expanding; nevertheless, this fact is a reminder not to fantasize about early Christian gatherings as being utopian. Clearly, something attractive was going on, or else they wouldn't have grown so powerfully and quickly across the empire. But we get a strong sense that that growth happened *despite* conflict, rivalry, and tensions, not in the absence of them.

*They did not protest the institution of slavery.* In the modern era of history, it is sometimes claimed that Christians like William Wilberforce advocated for the abolition of slavery thanks to their Christian convictions about the inherent dignity and freedom of people as precious creatures made by God. The same cannot be said of the first Christians, who did not question the Roman system of slavery and in many ways reinforced it. On the one hand, the apostle Paul boldly states, "There is no longer slave or free" (Gal. 3:28), but he also tells the Corinthians that each believer should not change their status in their remaining time on earth. The uncircumcised should not seek circumcision. Slaves? Paul counsels that if manumission (legal freedom) is a possibility, then they should go ahead and avail themselves of it. Otherwise, they should remain content (1 Cor. 7:21–23) because "freedom" can be found in Christ even while someone is a slave. "In whatever condition you were called, brothers and sisters, there remain with God" (7:24). You can see here that Paul opens the door for freedom for slaves, but this is a far cry from criticism of the institution itself.

On top of that, we must reckon with the household codes, the several places in the New Testament where obedience is demanded of Christian slaves. In Ephesians and Colossians, slaves are told to obey their masters with their whole heart (Eph. 6:5–6; Col. 3:22). Another text warns slaves not to talk back to masters (Titus 2:9). First Peter makes it explicit that a slave ought to accept the authority of even a cruel master (1 Pet. 2:18). Now, it is true that in all these texts, masters are told to treat slaves with respect, fairness, and sobriety. But again, at no point is it mentioned that slaves should not be slaves and masters should not be masters.

We have already talked about the intriguing situation of the master Philemon and the slave Onesimus, the only early Christian text with a sole focus on this kind of relationship. Paul invests deeply in Onesimus and advocates strongly for him. He wants Philemon to welcome Onesimus back with warmth and hospitality. He exhorts Philemon to accept him as "more than a slave," as a beloved brother in Christ (Philem. 16). That posture toward a slave—someone often treated in the Roman world as merely a personal possession—is remarkable and says something about the possibilities of social transformation within the Christian vision for community. However, at no point does Paul say that Onesimus deserves care and concern *simply as a fellow human being,* and Paul does not explicitly pressure Philemon to grant Onesimus his freedom.[1]

Now, a convenient explanation could be that slavery was simply taken for granted, and perhaps the thought of no more slavery simply never occurred to people at that time. But in fact, there were groups that actively rejected slavery as a social evil. The Essenes, a Jewish community, are described as people who possessed no slaves, because slavery bred injustice.[2] Why didn't the Christians also take this kind of stand? Some have said that the apostles imagined that the end of the world was happening imminently, so there was no point. But even in the Christian writings of the second, third, and fourth centuries, we still find that Christians simply took slavery for granted and that they were more than comfortable with it and reinforced the notion that Christian slaves should be on their best behavior.[3]

*They slandered each other and used judgmental speech.* The early Christians talked a lot about love; in fact, that was a clear distinctive of their discourse. God is love in himself, so Christians ought to overflow with love for each other and for all. The emphasis on love is found in nearly every New Testament text. And yet, for all this gushing about love, Jesus and the apostles made a lot of harsh statements about certain fellow Jews and other peoples, accusing them of doing evil and condemning groups to damnation.[4] For example, in the Gospel of John, Jesus rebukes the Jews he is talking with, claiming, "You are from your father the devil, and you choose to do your father's desires. He was a murderer from the beginning and does not stand in the truth, because there is no truth in him" (John 8:44). In the book of Acts, Peter gives a speech to a group of Jews. He addresses them as "Israelites" and confronts them by making the accusation "you crucified" Jesus of Nazareth (Acts 2:22–23). Texts like these have been read throughout the years as Christians putting the blame for the death of God on Jews, and people have concluded that the Jews as a whole deserve damnation. This is a concept know as Jewish "deicide" (accusing the Jewish people of the murder of God), which most Christians throughout history and today would not identify with. However, there are numerous statements in the New Testament that blame Jews for the death of Christ and claim some sort of divine retribution. For instance, Paul comforts the (mostly Gentile) Thessalonian believers in their suffering by pointing to divine judgment on the persecutors: "For you, brothers and sisters, became imitators of the churches of God in Christ Jesus that are in Judea, for you suffered the same things from your own compatriots as they did from the Jews, who killed both the Lord Jesus and the prophets, and drove us out; they displease God and oppose everyone by hindering us from speaking to the Gentiles so that they may be saved. Thus they have constantly been filling up the measure of their sins; but God's wrath has overtaken them at last" (1 Thess. 2:14–16).

Again, in such texts Jews are being blamed for killing Jesus and his followers. God is upset with these Jews, and God's wrath will lead to their damnation. I have tried to make sense of why Paul would write this, but even if we could find some innocent reasoning, such strongly worded statements have fueled Christian anti-Semitism throughout the years, and those reverberations and shockwaves are still felt today.[5] Now, in the middle of the first century, Christianity was very small, a few thousand people across a vast empire. Some of these texts, like 1 Thessalonians, were private correspondences that were not meant for public consumption. Today we might write something in a private text that we would never post on social media, and Paul likewise might have written things in private correspondence that he would have been more careful about publicly. But the reality is that these early Christian texts *were* collected and circulated widely without disclaimers and explanatory notes. And eventually, they became part of sacred Scripture—such words of judgment now the Word of God. I wonder if Paul would have edited his speech if he had known that millions upon millions of people would read his words. Consideration should probably be given to the fact that the early Christians were going against the grain of respectable religion in the Roman world and were distinguishing themselves from Jews and traditional Jewish religion as well. That may have motivated some of these incendiary statements. But this does not justify them, nor does it undo the great damage done by Christians over the centuries who have treated Jews as the enemies of God rather than covenantal forebears.

I believe the first Christians were stepping into a whole new way of knowing God, of engaging in religion, and of thinking about the world. I think they deviated from the norm and opened the known world up to new ideas, many of them with the potential to do great things for society. But they were far from perfect. I don't think it's absurd to claim a sense of exceptionalism for a group of people. Yet it becomes intellectually dishonest and, frankly, dangerous when we hide the limitations, mistakes, or downsides of that group or movement. Nothing is gained by creating a false history, and much is lost. I think Christians can claim that the gospel of Jesus is completely true with a clean conscience, but there must be some acceptance of human failing when it comes to the behavior of all Christians, including early Christians.

In the last chapter of this book, we will pull together a final synthesis of this strange religion and think a bit about how the church can hold true to its best ideals of religion, personal formation, and contributions toward the common good today.

# Strange Religion

*Putting It All Together*

W e circle back now to pull together the different threads of this book to see what key themes and ideas emerge. Not all first-century churches were the same. Christians disagreed then in many of the same ways they do now: about theology, worship styles, lifestyle, culture, politics. But to the extent that I can paint with broad brushstrokes (a necessary but difficult practice of historians), I will attempt to provide a synthesis of what made the early Christians weird.

## A People Obsessed with Jesus

This is an obvious one, but perhaps it deserves repeating because it would have been so noticeable to pagan visitors of early Christian assemblies. I am not sure what a visitor would have guessed about how many gods Christians worshiped, but what would have been clear was that these people were obsessed with Jesus. The name "Jesus" (alone) appears about nine hundred times in the New Testament; the combination "Jesus Christ" or "Christ Jesus" appears about two hundred times. So Jesus comes up about once every eight verses on average. Jesus was not just the center of Christian religion; he was the center of the Christians' lives. Romans 14:7–9 captures this well: "We do not live to ourselves, and we do not die to ourselves. If we live, we live to the Lord, and if we die, we die to the Lord; so then, whether we live or whether we die, we are the Lord's. For to this end Christ died and lived again, so that he might be Lord of both the dead and the living."

It is true that in the ancient world all people participated in religion. All people saw honoring the gods as part of their civic duty to ensure their welfare and the welfare of their community. So in that sense everyone was religious. But these Christians were *really* religious. An average Roman couldn't have a conversation with a Christian without Jesus coming up. "Jesus" this and "Jesus" that. All things belonged to the Lord.

I think this would have resembled, in some ways, the passions of mystery-cult worshipers, who were more driven by emotional attachment to a deity than the average Roman. Or perhaps this was like Roman Ephesus's overall attachment to the goddess Artemis. It seemed like the whole city revolved around this local cult. Christians took it one step further than most other cults by claiming absolute supremacy for Jesus. He was the master agent of creation, he ruled supreme over all, and he would be judge of the cosmos in the future. These were grand claims, to say the least. One might have heard such things said about Jupiter ("Best and Greatest"!) and, to some degree, the emperor as the mortal agent executing divine justice. But the Christian claims were absolute. There was no competitive hierarchy of the gods. God (the Father) and Jesus (the Son of God) operated in unity, and Jesus actually became human to save humanity; he was even willing to die on a cross of shame. For this act of generosity, Jesus was highly exalted by the Father and venerated by Christians. To say this about a cult from a foreign land (Judea) would have been unusual, even off-putting for most Romans. To say this about a criminal who had been condemned to die a slave's death would have been an offense and an abomination not even worth entertaining. But these people honored Jesus and claimed for him resurrection and supreme lordship.

## Mind on the Future

Whenever my family is expecting company at our house, we go into preparation mode, especially if they are going to spend the night. We create a checklist of necessary cleaning, a shopping list for meals, and we plan out some recipes. Our minds become preoccupied with something important that will be happening in the future—more specifically, something that is coming to *us*. That is, in a sense, how the Christians were behaving. Their lives were preoccupied with the future. Christ ascended into heaven; he promised to come back, and in the meantime the people were meant to be ready. *Vigilance.* That did not mean disengagement with the "now" time and the things of this world. Paul, for example, reminded the Thessalonians of the importance of putting their hands to good use and living a "quiet" life (1 Thess. 4:11). That meant daily rhythms of labor and peaceable contributions to society. An "eschatological" theology did not mean standing on a street corner with a sign saying "The end of the world is near." (If Christians did stand on a corner with a sign, it would probably say "Ask me about Jesus.")

Ancient religions, by and large, didn't dwell on the future, certainly not with any kind of specificity. Religion was primarily about maintaining the traditions of worship that had been passed down from ancestors and that ensured the blessing of the gods. Jews and Christians, however, were dedicated to lengthy Scriptures that outlined promises of God about future vindication and renewal.

## A Religion of the Heart

I am struck by the sheer number of times that the early Christian writings talk about the heart, the interior life of the worshiper. The God of the Christians did not just want the correct performance of certain rituals, or the profession of fidelity through oaths. This God wanted genuine faith, even love. Here are a series of statements from the New Testament that relate to the heart:

> So [Jesus] said to them, "You are those who justify yourselves in the sight of others; but God knows your hearts; for what is prized by human beings is an abomination in the sight of God." (Luke 16:15)

> [God] knows the human heart. (Acts 15:8)

> [God] searches the heart. (Rom. 8:27)

> The Lord . . . will bring to light the things now hidden in darkness and will disclose the purposes of the heart. (1 Cor. 4:5)

> I pray that . . . [the Father] may grant that you may be strengthened in your inner being with power through his Spirit, and that Christ may dwell in your hearts through faith. (Eph. 3:16–17)

> And the peace of God, which surpasses all understanding, will guard your hearts and your minds in Christ Jesus. (Phil. 4:7)

> God . . . tests our hearts. (1 Thess. 2:4)

> The word of God is living and active, sharper than any two-edged sword, piercing until it divides soul from spirit, joints

208

from marrow; it is able to judge the thoughts and intentions of the heart. (Heb. 4:12)

If any think they are religious, and do not bridle their tongues but deceive their hearts, their religion is worthless. (James 1:26)

In your hearts set apart Christ as Lord. (1 Pet. 3:15, my trans.)

I am the one who searches minds and hearts. (Rev. 2:23)

There are many more texts like this; this is just a small sampling. But I am struck by the consistency across the several New Testament authors. They largely believe the same thing, that the life of religion ultimately comes down to belief, trust, love, and action that must be genuine, that begins in the inner life. Rote ritualism and half-hearted worship isn't going to cut it. God perceives heart and soul. He knows genuine faith from artificial piety.

This Christian emphasis on heart and soul draws from Jewish tradition. As mentioned in chapter 2, God explains to the prophet Samuel, "Do not look on [David's brother Eliab's] appearance or on the height of his stature, because I have rejected him; for the Lord does not see as mortals see; they look on the outward appearance, but the Lord looks on the heart" (1 Sam. 16:7). This affirmation of the God of Israel as the heart-seer is ingrained in Jewish liturgy. "Search me, O God, and know my heart," the psalmist prays. "Test me and know my thoughts. See if there is any wicked way in me, and lead me in the way everlasting" (Ps. 139:23–24). And Israel's most famous prayer-creed says, "Hear, O Israel: The Lord is our God, the Lord alone. You shall love the Lord your God with all your heart, and with all your soul, and with all your might" (Deut. 6:4–5). This God wants obedience from Israel, but it must come from the heart. It cannot be mere words or thoughtless actions.

Jesus often taught on this notion that real and lasting change can come only from inner transformation, because behavior follows belief and the intentions of the heart. "No good tree bears bad fruit, nor again does a bad tree bear good fruit; for each tree is known by its own fruit. . . . The good person out of the good treasure of the heart produces good, and the evil person out of evil treasure produces evil; for it is out of the abundance of the heart that the mouth speaks" (Luke 6:43–45). In his lessons, Jesus often sounded more like a moral philosopher than a classic priest. He cared deeply about realizing a vision for a new world, a world filled with goodness and love. That vision inspired his followers and left a deep impact on those whom we would later call Christians.

## A "God-with-Us" Religion

Roman religion saw the realm of the gods as distinct from the mortal plane. Human and divine lived within one cosmos, but the gods did not roam around freely on earth. They would visit once in a while, but they had their home elsewhere. The earth had a number of hotspots where mortals could interface with the gods: temples, sacred groves, shrines, and cult statues— and some occasionally connected with the gods through ecstatic experiences. But by and large, worshipers had to locate a bridge or door between worlds to encounter the divine. Christians had the incredible belief that the one God wanted to be with people on earth. Drawing from Jewish tradition, they believed that when sin entered the world, it caused a great breech between heaven and earth. God was no longer at home on the earth. He visited the earth as a stranger. In the era of Moses and later on during the period of the monarchy, Israel was given three key tools for engaging in their covenant with

God: the temple (the space of meeting), the law (the revealed will of God), and the kingdom (the institution through which God ruled his people). These were sturdy and effective tools, but they did not indicate the full and intimate presence of God on earth. The temple could be destroyed, the law could be disobeyed, and the kingdom could be fractured. Israel longed for the fulfillment of God's promises to live among the people on earth as he had in the garden of Eden (see Isa. 40:9). Eventually, some Jews put their hope in a royal figure, a Jewish Messiah, who would embody God's rule on earth (Ezek. 34:23–24).

The Gospel of John points to Jesus as that eschatological figure: the Good Shepherd who leads and guides his people; the way of God, the truth of God, and the life of God; the Word who took on the flesh of humanity to live among the people (John 1:14). In the Gospel of Matthew, when an angel tells Joseph about the holy pregnancy of Mary, the angel announces the fulfillment of Isaiah 7:14:

> "Look, the virgin shall conceive and bear a son,
>    and they shall name him Emmanuel,"
> which means, "God is with us." (Matt. 1:23)

In the days of the prophet Isaiah, those who first heard this pronouncement were probably imagining a great human king, like David but even better, who would be so righteous and holy that it would seem as though God himself were ruling. The story of Jesus goes far beyond this—Jesus is both human and divine, a good shepherd and *the* Good Shepherd. God is near. This is the realization of the hopes of Israel expressed in Isaiah 64:1: "O that you would tear open the heavens and come down!" In a sense Jesus's presence was temporary. He died on a cross, was buried, rose again, then ascended into heaven. But the situation after was not like the situation before. He ascended to rule earth from heaven, and the Spirit was sent

211

to spread the presence of God across the whole world. This initiated that religious "technology" innovation, where a worshiper no longer needed to go to a hotspot to commune with the divine, to touch heaven and have heaven touch earth. Now every believer had a "signal" within themselves (1 Cor. 6:19). This was not just a religious convenience. It said something about this God. Not only did he not mind being "bothered" by mortals; he pursued them. He cared deeply about them, so much so that he wanted to be with them all the time. "God with us" had to do with "God loves us."

## From *Pax Deorum* (Peace with the Gods) to *Caritas Dei* (Love of God)

The above concept leads naturally to the Christian emphasis on the love of God, which refers both to the love God has for people and the love people are meant to have for God. I have tried to make it clear in this book that that would have come across as weird to most Romans. Roman religion was focused on *pax deorum*, maintaining civil peace with the gods. The framework that was often used was that of politics. The gods were like human kings, lords, and magistrates. They wanted service, obedience, and commitment to duty. The subjects wanted fair treatment, reasonable taxes, and some entertainment every now and then if it wasn't too much trouble ("bread and circuses" and all that). Love never really factored into the equation any more than we would use "love" language in modern politics and civic duty today. I don't love paying taxes; I know it's proper, and I do it because it's fair, but it's not something I get very emotional about. But what we see in the discourses of the early Christians is a shift from the paradigm of governance to the paradigm of family. God was a loving Father who wanted to take care of his children (Matt. 7:11; Luke 11:13). The religious community was first and foremost not an association or cult but, rather, a household of love and belonging. It was still a place of respect and order, but the family paradigm was meant to create a context of warmth, intimacy, friendship, and grace. The people came together not to seek peace but to express and exchange love with the God who initiated peace (Eph. 2:17).

## The Church as a Utopian Community

The word "utopia" comes from the Greek prefix *eu-* (meaning "good") and *topos* (meaning "place"): a good place. When we read the New Testament, the earliest Christian literature, it is clear that the first Christians sought to assemble a virtuous, loving community of mutuality, honor, and goodness. We have already talked about how these early Christians were not perfect. They bickered. They struggled with unity. They sometimes undermined one another. But in their best moments, you see a beautiful family of faith.

The Romans had Saturnalia, the popular winter festival that imitated a long-past golden age. During the celebration, slaves pretended to be masters, and masters took orders from slaves. It was lots of good fun, but it was indeed pretend, and when the festival was done, the roles returned to normal. Christians carried a more permanent vision of a "good place." No more judging people by ethnicity (Jew or Gentile), social status (slave or free), or gender (biological sex). The person who normally would have sat in the back was to sit in the front, and vice versa. Children were important and were to be welcomed, not shooed away. No one was to have more money or resources if that meant that someone else had too little; God willed that each person had just what they needed. Utopia indeed. The early Christians were ambitious enough. Apparently they even tried to live without property or possessions, pooling their resources into one pot. That didn't stick, but they were trying to realize Jesus's vision for establishing a microcosm of heaven on earth. The gospel they preached wasn't just about religious observances or opportunities to commune with the divine. It was about the possibility of a whole world transformed toward goodness, charity, peace, joy, and prosperity.

*Weird.* There's no getting around the fact that Christians deviated from common and public Roman religion. There would be natural similarities—worship, respect for the divine, prayers for blessing, commitment to traditions, prophecy. But the differences are notable and many. A Roman visiting a Christian assembly would have found much of what was going on confusing. "Where are the priests and sacrifices? Who is this Jesus Christ? Why are there no cult statues around? What is Scripture? What is the day of Christ?" Many visitors would have left feeling discomfort.

*Dangerous.* One person's "weird" is another person's "dangerous." "These Christians go too far! The way they talk about this Jesus—a criminal, by the way—makes him out to be the highest being in the universe. That kind of talk threatens the cosmic order. Jupiter is 'Best and Greatest.' And Lord Caesar is the greatest earthly being!" Rome tolerated a lot of weird stuff. Foreign cults were permitted, though popular ones were monitored closely. But some would have thought that these Christians took weird to a whole other level, that they took it too far. Their obsession with Jesus smacked of *superstitio.* Romans believed that proper religion had certain rules and boundaries to protect the people from offending the gods and inviting wrath. *Superstitio* was a label used for aberrant forms of *religio.* Christian religion violated so many religious norms that it was inevitable some would consider it a threat to civic order.

*Compelling.* And yet we know that it drew interest and grew exponentially. Why did that happen? Some say it was the promise of immortality. Some say it was the networking

214

savvy of spreading the religion in an organized way across the whole empire. Some say it was the attraction of monotheism. Some say it was the teaching on morality. I am sure all of these are factors. But I can't help but believe it was *the people*, the Christians themselves. In the first century a Roman encounter with Jesus was probably going to happen through a small community of Christians. This community had to be compelling.

## What Color Is Christianity Really?

I began this book with an analogy from coconut water. Surprise, surprise, it's pink! While some manufacturers want to sell a clear drink to people, offering the impression of refreshing purity, there are people who are okay with weird color tones. This book is my attempt to examine early Christianity as it was according to our best records and within their own religious, social, and cultural context. There's no getting around that the early Christians were different and unexpected, off-putting to

Fresh coconut water

some but attractive and compelling to others. The first Jesus followers were okay with being different, deviating from the status quo, following Jesus and his way wherever that went. Perhaps there is a need today for the modern church to pick up a bottle of their religion and say, "Hey, that looks different, but good and refreshing things sometimes come from weird places."

# Notes

## Chapter 1  Roman Religion and the *Pax Deorum*

1. Numa Denis Fustel de Coulanges, *The Ancient City: A Study on the Religion, Laws, and Institutes of Greece and Rome* (Baltimore: Johns Hopkins University Press, 1980), 146.

2. Pliny, *Natural History* 2.5.16; trans. John Bostock, *The Natural History of Pliny* (London: Henry G. Bohn, 1855), 21. See also Cicero, *On the Nature of the Gods* 1.84; Petronius, *The Satyricon* 17.5.

3. Mary Beard, *The Fires of Vesuvius: Pompeii Lost and Found* (Cambridge, MA: Harvard University Press, 2008), 276.

4. John Scheid, *An Introduction to Roman Religion* (Edinburgh: Edinburgh University Press, 2003), 147.

5. *On the Nature of the Gods* 2.8.

6. *On the Nature of the Gods* 1.116.

7. See Robert Turcan, *The Gods of Ancient Rome: Religion in Everyday Life from Archaic to Imperial Times* (New York: Routledge, 2001), 5.

8. Plautus, *Bacchides* 144; quoted in Valerie Warrior, *Roman Religion* (Cambridge: Cambridge University Press, 2006), 1.

9. Warrior, *Roman Religion*, 1.

10. *The Iliad of Homer*, trans. Alexander Pope (Edinburgh: James Hunter, 1792), book 24, lines 525–33, p. 476.

11. Porphyry, *On Abstinence* 2.16; as depicted in John Ferguson, *Greek and Roman Religion: A Source Book* (Park Ridge, NJ: Noyes, 1980), 60.

12. See Turcan, *Gods of Ancient Rome*.

13. My translation of Plautus, *Amphitryon* 1–25; based on Mary Beard, John North, and Simon R. F. Price, *Religions of Rome* (Cambridge: Cambridge University Press, 1998), 2:29.

14. Cicero, *On the Nature of the Gods* 3.87–89; trans. Warrior, *Roman Religion*, 9.

15. Plautus, *Merchant* 678–79; Valerius Maximus, *Memorable Deeds and Sayings* 2.5.6.

16. Suetonius, *Gaius Caligula* 5.2.
17. Valerius Maximus, *Memorable Deeds and Sayings* 2.5.6; quoted in Warrior, *Roman Religion*, 4.
18. Servius, *Commentary on the Aeneid* 2.351; see Nicole Belayche, "Religious Actors in Daily Life: Practice and Related Beliefs," in *A Companion to Roman Religion*, ed. Jörg Rüpke (Malden, MA: Blackwell, 2007), 279–80; Turcan, *Gods of Ancient Rome*, 4.
19. Belayche, "Religious Actors," 281.
20. In Latin, *Iuppiter Optimus Maximus*; see Julia Hejduk, *The God of Rome: Jupiter in Augustan Poetry* (Oxford: Oxford University Press, 2010).
21. Beard, *Fires of Vesuvius*, 279–80.
22. See Philip Kiernan, *Roman Cult Images: The Lives and Worship of Idols, from the Iron Age to Late Antiquity* (Cambridge: Cambridge University Press, 2020), 6.
23. Jörg Rüpke, *On Roman Religion: Lived Religion and the Individual in Ancient Rome* (New York: Cornell University Press, 2016), 8.

## Chapter 2 "Believers"

1. Mary Beard, *The Fires of Vesuvius: Pompeii Lost and Found* (Cambridge, MA: Harvard University Press, 2008), 278.
2. Clifford Ando, *The Matter of the Gods: Religion and the Roman Empire* (Berkeley: University of California Press, 2008), 13.
3. Robert Turcan, *The Gods of Ancient Rome: Religion in Everyday Life from Archaic to Imperial Times* (New York: Routledge, 2001), 3.
4. Turcan, *Gods of Ancient Rome*, 2.
5. Nicole Belayche, "Religious Actors in Daily Life: Practice and Related Beliefs," in *A Companion to Roman Religion*, ed. Jörg Rüpke (Malden, MA: Blackwell, 2007), 279. Belayche also explains, "Ritualism is *the* relational procedure that fits coherently with the way Romans conceived the respective places of men and gods within the world" (291). See also George Heyman: "*Religio* was the proper *behavior* that characterized the life of the Roman citizen. Roman religion was not concerned with distinguishing *true* from *false* beliefs. It was more correctly understood as an existential category, discerning the proper actions that would ensure the success of the people and the state." Heyman, *The Power of Sacrifice: Roman and Christian Discourses in Conflict* (Washington, DC: Catholic University of America Press, 2007), 12.
6. Veit Roseberger, "Republican *Nobiles*: Controlling the *Res Publica*," in Rüpke, *Companion to Roman Religion*, 292–303, here 300.
7. Virgil explains that prayers alone are futile if the ritual is performed wrong (*Georgics* 3.454); see Turcan, *Gods of Ancient Rome*, 11. Plutarch himself argues that one's mind and heart ought to align with one's religious actions and oaths, but he complains that "the mass of mankind" swear by the gods, but then speak ill of the same gods. Plutarch, "Isis and Osiris," in *Moralia*, vol. 5, trans. F. C. Babbitt, LCL 306 (Cambridge, MA: Harvard University Press, 1936), 159.

8. See more detailed argument in my book *Paul and the Language of Faith* (Grand Rapids: Eerdmans, 2020).

9. Josephus, *Against Apion* 2.148; Cassius Dio, *Roman History* 67.14; *Martyrdom of Polycarp* 3.2; Eusebius, *Ecclesiastical History* 3.13; Lucian of Samosata, *Peregrinus* 13; Porphyry, *Against the Christians* 1.2.3.

10. Josephus, *Jewish Antiquities* 14.68–78; Tacitus, *History* 5.9.

11. Tacitus, *History* 5.9; trans. Alfred John Church and William Jackson Brodribb, *The Complete Works of Tacitus* (London: Macmillan, 1905), 539.

12. Philo, *Flaccus* 1.41–51; see the discussion by Paul V. M. Flesher, "Prolegomenon to the Theory of Early Synagogue Development," in *Judaism in Late Antiquity: The Special Problem of the Synagogue*, ed. Alan J. Avery-Peck and Jacob Neusner (Boston: Brill, 2001), 121–54.

13. Michael Green, *Evangelism in the Early Church* (Grand Rapids: Eerdmans, 2004), 43. Green here quotes Tacitus, *The Histories*, vol. 2, 5.9 (trans. W. Hamilton Fyfe [Oxford: Clarendon, 1912], 213).

14. Josephus, *Jewish Antiquities* 3.6.

15. See Jacob L. Mackey, *Belief and Cult: Rethinking Roman Religion* (Princeton: Princeton University Press, 2022).

## Chapter 3  A Dangerous and Strange Religon

1. Pausanias, describing Athens, mentions "altars of the gods named Unknown" (*bōmoi theōn te onomazomenōn Agnōstōn*; *Description of Greece* 1.1.4); similarly, 5.14.8 mentions "an altar of unknown gods" (*Agnōstōn theōn bōmos*) in Elis in the Peloponnese. Diogenes Laertius writes that "even to this day altars may be found in different parts of Attica with no name inscribed upon them" (*kai nyn estin heurein kata tous dēmous tōn Athēnaiōn bōmous anōnymous*; *Lives* 1.110). Philostratus advises speaking well of every god, especially at Athens, "where even altars of unknown gods are set up" (*hou kai agnōstōn daimonōn bōmoi hidryntai*; *Life of Apollonius* 6.3); all quoted in Carl R. Holladay, *Acts: A Commentary*, New Testament Library (Louisville: Westminster John Knox, 2016), 343–44.

2. See Tim Whitmarsh, *Battling the Gods: Atheism in the Ancient World* (New York: Knopf, 2015), 20; Gregory S. Aldrete, *Daily Life in the Roman City: Rome, Pompeii, and Ostia* (Westport, CT: Greenwood, 2004), 142–43; Robert Turcan, *The Gods of Ancient Rome: Religion in Everyday Life from Archaic to Imperial Times* (New York: Routledge, 2001), 2.

3. Xenophon, *Memorabilia* 1.1.1; Plato, *Apology* 24B; see Josephus, *Jewish Antiquities* 2.265–67; Euripides, *Bacchae* 255; Donald R. Morrison, "Socrates," in *A Companion to Ancient Philosophy*, ed. Sean D. Kirkland and Eric Sanday (Evanston, IL: Northwestern University Press, 2018), 101–18.

4. See Mary Beard, John North, and Simon R. F. Price, *Religions of Rome* (Cambridge: Cambridge University Press, 1998), 1:211–44.

5. George Heyman, *The Power of Sacrifice: Roman and Christian Discourses in Conflict* (Washington, DC: Catholic University of America Press, 2007), 12.

6. "Leave Fireworks to the Professionals," Mass.gov, https://www.mass.gov /service-details/leave-fireworks-to-the-professionals.

7. Beard, North, and Price, *Religions of Rome*, 1:221.

8. Josephus, *Jewish Antiquities* 1.5–9.

9. Valerius Maximus, *Memorable Deeds and Sayings* 2.1.1; see Nicole Belayche, "Religious Actors in Daily Life: Practice and Related Beliefs," in *A Companion to Roman Religion*, ed. Jörg Rüpke (Malden, MA: Blackwell, 2007), 278; John Scheid, *An Introduction to Roman Religion* (Bloomington: Indiana University Press, 2003), 22–23.

10. Beard, North, and Price, *Religions of Rome*, 2:217.

11. Quoted in Hans-Josef Klauck, *The Religious Context of Early Christianity: A Guide to the Graeco-Roman Religions* (Edinburgh: T&T Clark, 2000), 62; see also Jennifer Cianca, *Sacred Ritual, Profane Space: The Roman House as Early Christian Meeting Place* (Chicago: McGill-Queen's University Press, 2018), 61.

12. Philostratus, *Life of Apollonius* 6.16.

13. Matthew W. Dickie, *Magic and Magicians in the Greco-Roman World* (New York: Routledge, 2001); John Granger Cook, *Crucifixion in the Mediterranean World* (Tübingen: Mohr Siebeck, 2014), 393–94.

14. Jörg Rüpke, "*Religio* and *Religiones* in Roman Thinking," *Les Études Classiques* 75 (2007): 67–78: "*Religio* is not a vague feeling or an 'empty fear' like *superstitio*, but something resulting from the acceptance of the gods as part of one's social order, a human disposition, a habit, that finds its expression in corresponding rituals" (68).

15. Turcan, *Gods of Ancient Rome*, 10.

16. Turcan, *Gods of Ancient Rome*, 11.

17. George Heyman, *The Power of Sacrifice: Roman and Christian Discourses in Conflict* (Washington, DC: Catholic University of America Press, 2007), 12.

18. See Turcan, *Gods of Ancient Rome*, 5; Tacitus, *Histories* 5.13.1

19. See Dieter Mitternacht, "Current Views on the Synagogue of Ostia Antica and the Jews of Rome and Ostia," in *The Ancient Synagogue: From Its Origins until 200 CE*, ed. Birger Olsson and Magnus Zetterholm, Coniectanea Biblica, New Testament Series 39 (Stockholm: Almqvist & Wiksell, 2003), 521–71; Sten Hidal, "The Jews as the Romans Saw Them," in *The Synagogue of Ancient Ostia and the Jews of Rome: Interdisciplinary Studies*, ed. Birger Olsson, Dieter Mitternacht, and Olof Brandt (Stockholm: Paul Aströms, 2001), 141–44.

20. Patrick Miller, *The Ten Commandments*, Interpretation (Louisville: Westminster John Knox, 2009), 15–21.

21. Josephus, *Against Apion* 2.76–77.

22. Josephus, *Jewish War* 2.197; cf. Josephus, *Jewish Antiquities* 11.17, 102.

23. Quintilian, *Institutes of Oratory* 3.7.2.

24. Trans. Peter Schäfer, *Judeophobia: Attitudes toward the Jews in the Ancient World* (Cambridge, MA: Harvard University Press, 1998), 182; see Philo, *Against Flaccus* 69.

25. Plutarch, *On Superstition* 8.

26. Plutarch, *On Superstition* 9, in *Moralia*, vol. 2, trans. Frank Cole Babbitt (Cambridge, MA: Harvard University Press, 1928), 483.

27. Paraphrase from Plutarch, *On Superstition* 10.

28. Aldrete, *Daily Life in the Roman City*, 163.

29. Tacitus, *Annals* 15.44.

30. Tacitus, *Annals* 15.44; quoted in Beard, North, and Price, *Religions of Rome*, 2:277

31. Pliny, *Letters* 10.9–10; quoted in Beard, North, and Price, *Religions of Rome*, 2:277.

32. John M. G. Barclay, "'Jews' and 'Christians' in the Eyes of Roman Authors c. 100 CE," in *Jews and Christians in the First and Second Centuries: How to Write Their History*, ed. P. J. Tomson and J. Schwartz (Leiden: Brill, 2014), 313–26.

33. Suetonius, *Lives of the Caesars*, vol. 2, trans. J. C. Rolfe, LCL (Cambridge, MA: Harvard University Press, 1914), 107; see also Barclay, "'Jews' and 'Christians,'" 317.

34. See Aldrete, *Daily Life in the Roman City*; Michael Lipka, *Roman Gods: A Conceptual Approach* (Boston: Brill, 2009).

## Chapter 4 Believing the Unbelievable

1. For a thorough discussion, see Felicity Harley-McGowan, "The Alexamenos Graffito," in *From Celsus to the Catacombs: Visual, Liturgical, and Non-Christian Receptions of Jesus in the Second and Third Centuries*, ed. C. Keith et al., vol. 3, *The Reception of Jesus in the First Three Centuries* (London: T&T Clark, 2020), 141–50.

2. See Mary R. Lefkowitz, *Greek Gods, Human Lives: What We Can Learn from Myths* (New Haven: Yale University Press, 2003), 13–29.

3. See John Scheid, "Hierarchy and Structure in Roman Polytheism: Roman Methods of Conceiving Action," in *Roman Religion*, ed. Clifford Ando (Edinburgh: Edinburgh University Press, 2003), 164–89.

4. Mary Beard, John North, and Simon R. F. Price, *Religions of Rome* (Cambridge: Cambridge University Press, 1998), 2:41.

5. Livy, *History* 5.21.1–7; quoted in Beard, North, and Price, *Religions of Rome*, 2:42.

6. See also Epictetus, *Discourse* 4.1.12; Plutarch, *Brutus* 30.3.

7. See Joseph D. Fantin, *Lord of the Entire World: Lord Jesus, A Challenge to Lord Caesar?* (Sheffield: Sheffield Phoenix, 2011), 152. Fantin discusses these sources: "lord god Cronos" (Orientis Graeci Inscriptiones Selectae 606); "lord god Soknopaios" (Papyrus Tebtynis [Arsinoites] 284.5–6); "lord Sarapis" (Oxyrhynchus Papyri 523.1–3).

8. See David Capes, *The Divine Christ: Paul, the Lord Jesus, and the Scriptures of Israel* (Grand Rapids: Baker Academic, 2018), and Chris Tilling, *Paul's Divine Christology* (Grand Rapids: Eerdmans, 2012).

9. Fantin notes one occasion, in Pindar, where Zeus is hailed "lord of all" (*Isthmean Odes* 5.53); Fantin, *Lord of the Entire World*, 139.

10. See Fantin, *Lord of the Entire World*, 190–96.

11. S. R. F. Price, *Rituals and Power: The Roman Imperial Cult in Asia Minor* (Cambridge: Cambridge University Press, 1984), 233; quoted in C. Kavin Rowe, "Luke-Acts and the Imperial Cult: A Way through the Conundrum," *Journal for the Study of the New Testament* 27, no. 3 (2005): 279–300, here 298.

12. The Greek text here is terse: *di ou ta panta kai hēmeis di autou*. A wooden translation would be "through whom all things and we through him."

13. Seneca, "On Mercy," in *Moral Essays*, trans. John Basore, LCL 214 (Cambridge, MA: Harvard University Press, 1928), 357.

14. For the importance of this prayer in early Judaism, see Richard Bauckham, "The Shema and 1 Corinthians 8.6 Again," in *One God, One People, One Future: Essays in Honor of N. T. Wright*, ed. John Anthony Dunne and Eric Lewellen (Minneapolis: Fortress, 2018), 86–111.

15. N. T. Wright, "One God, One Lord: How Paul Redefines Monotheism," *Christian Century* (November 27, 2013), 23.

16. Wright, "One God, One Lord," 23.

17. John Bowden and Martin Hengel, *Crucifixion in the Ancient World and the Folly of the Message of the Cross* (Philadelphia: Fortress, 1977); John Granger Cook, *Crucifixion in the Mediterranean World*, 2nd ed. (Tübingen: Mohr Siebeck, 2018).

18. David Wallace Chapman and Eckhard Schnabel, ed., *The Trial and Crucifixion of Jesus: Texts and Commentary* (Tübingen: Mohr Siebeck, 2015), 602.

### Chapter 5  Cult without Smoke and Blood

1. Hesiod, *Works and Days* 340–41; quoted in F. S. Naiden, *Smoke Signals for the Gods: Ancient Greek Sacrifice from the Archaic through the Roman Periods* (Oxford: Oxford University Press, 2013), 120.

2. Walter Brueggemann, *Worship in Ancient Israel* (Nashville: Abingdon, 2005), 11.

3. Mary Beard, *The Fires of Vesuvius: Pompeii Lost and Found* (Cambridge, MA: Harvard University Press, 2010), 292.

4. Ammianus Marcellinus, *Roman History* 15.4.16; quoted in Naiden, *Smoke Signals for the Gods*, 95.

5. Rebecca I. Denova, *Greek and Roman Religions* (Oxford: Blackwell, 2019), 17–18.

6. Plautus, *Pot of Gold* 621–23; quoted in Hans-Josef Klauck, *The Religious Context of Early Christianity: A Guide to the Graeco-Roman Religions* (Edinburgh: T&T Clark, 2000), 39.

7. Naiden, *Smoke Signals for the Gods*, 3–38.

8. M.-Z. Petropoulou, *Animal Sacrifice in Ancient Greek Religion, Judaism, and Christianity, 100 BC to AD 200* (Oxford: Oxford University Press, 2008), 141–42.

9. Josephus, *Against Apion* 2.76–77; *Jewish War* 2.197.

10. Beard, *Fires of Vesuvius*, 292.

11. For a detailed discussion, see M.-Z. Petropoulou, "Jewish Animal Sacrifice in the Period 100 BC–AD 200," in Petropoulou, *Animal Sacrifice*, 127–207.

12. Justin Martyr, *First Apology* 24–26; quoted and translated in Mary Beard, John North, and Simon R. F. Price, *Religions of Rome* (Cambridge: Cambridge University Press, 1998), 2:330.

13. Justin Martyr, *First Apology* 13, in *The Ante-Nicene Fathers*, trans. Alexander Roberts and James Donaldson (Buffalo: Christian Literature Company, 1884–86), 1:185.

14. Lee I. Levine, "Temple, Jerusalem," in *The Eerdmans Dictionary of Early Judaism*, ed. John J. Collins and Daniel C. Harlow (Grand Rapids: Eerdmans, 2010), 1289.

15. Oscar Cullmann, *Early Christian Worship* (London: SCM, 1950); Ralph Martin, *Worship in the Early Church* (Grand Rapids: Eerdmans, 1995); Paul Bradshaw, *Early Christian Worship: A Basic Introduction to Ideas and Practice* (Collegeville, MN: Liturgical Press, 1996).

16. See Richard Bauckham, *Jesus and the God of Israel* (Grand Rapids: Eerdmans, 2008), esp. 1–17, and Loren Stuckenbruck and Wendy E. S. North, ed., *Early Jewish and Christian Monotheism* (London: T&T Clark, 2004).

17. Marcus Aurelius, *Communings with Himself* 9.40; quoted and translated in Beard, North, and Price, *Religions of Rome*, 2:358.

18. See Matthew Dillon, *Omens and Oracles: Divination in Ancient Greece* (New York: Routledge, 2017), 329.

19. Ruth Mellinkoff, *The Horned Moses in Medieval Art and Thought* (Eugene, OR: Wipf & Stock, 1997).

20. G. K. Beale, *We Become What We Worship: A Biblical Theology of Idolatry* (Downers Grove, IL: IVP Academic, 2008), 79–86.

21. Naiden, *Smoke Signals for the Gods*, 287.

### Chapter 6 Possessed by the Spirit of God

1. David Frankfurter, "Traditional Cult," in *A Companion to the Roman Empire*, ed. David S. Potter (Malden, MA: Blackwell, 2006), 543–64, here 560.

2. See Philip Kiernan, *Roman Cult Images: The Lives and Worship of Idols, from the Iron Age to Late Antiquity* (Cambridge: Cambridge University Press, 2020), 147, and Hans-Josef Klauck, *The Religious Context of Early Christianity: A Guide to the Graeco-Roman Religions* (Edinburgh: T&T Clark, 2000), 26.

3. Mary Beard, *The Fires of Vesuvius: Pompeii Lost and Found* (Cambridge, MA: Harvard University Press, 2008), 285.

4. Josephus, *Against Apion* 2.193, in *The Works of Josephus: Complete and Unabridged*, trans. William Whiston (Peabody, MA: Hendrickson, 1987), 1147.

5. One might note as an exception the reference to the Man of Lawlessness taking residence in the temple and pretending to be the true God, before he is vanquished by Christ (2 Thess. 2:3–4). Paul also mentioned pagan temples (1 Cor. 9:13).

6. Michael Lipka, *Roman Gods: A Conceptual Approach* (Boston: Brill, 2009), 28.

7. Lipka, *Roman Gods*, 11.

8. See Catherine McDowell, *The Image of God in the Garden of Eden* (Winona Lake, IN: Eisenbrauns, 2015).

9. See Deborah Steiner, *Images in Mind: Statues in Archaic and Classical Greek Literature and Thought* (Princeton: Princeton University Press, 2001).

10. Much of the material in this section draws from the scholarship in my article "'They Are Not Gods!' Jewish and Christian Idol Polemic and Greco-Roman Use of Cult Statues," *Catholic Biblical Quarterly* 76 (2014): 704–19.

11. Pausanias, *Description* 6.11.2–9.

12. See Derek Collins, *Magic in the Ancient Greek World* (Oxford: Blackwell, 2008), 95.

13. See Donna C. Kurtz and John Boardman, *Greek Burial Customs* (Ithaca, NY: Cornell University Press, 1971), 247–59; also Sarah Iles Johnston, *Restless Dead: Encounters between the Living and the Dead in Ancient Greece* (Berkeley: University of California Press, 1999).

14. Nigel Spivey, "Bionic Statues," in *The Greek World*, ed. Anton Powell (London: Routledge, 1995), 442–62, here 445.

15. Strabo, *Geography* 6.1.14.

16. Dionysius of Halicarnassus, *Roman Antiquities* 8.56.2–3.

17. Dio Cassius, *Roman History* 46.33.4.

18. See Jörg Rüpke, *The Religions of the Romans* (Cambridge: Cambridge University Press, 2007), 74.

19. Diodorus Siculus, *Historical Library* 17.41.7–8; Plutarch, *Alexander* 24.5–8; Quintus Curtius Rufus, *The History of Alexander* 4.3.21–22.

20. John Barton, "Moral Agents and Moral Patients," in *Ethics in Ancient Israel* (Oxford: Oxford University Press, 2014), 41–76, here 64–65.

21. Plutarch, *Moralia* 580c–683b; quoted in Daniel Ogden, *Magic, Witchcraft, and Ghosts in the Greek and Roman Worlds: A Sourcebook* (Oxford: Oxford University Press, 2002), 222.

22. Horace, *Epistles* 1.14.37–38.

23. Ogden, *Magic, Witchcraft, and Ghosts,* 224.

24. It should be said, though, that the Spirit is involved in final judgment, but of the Spirit's own accord and not through the coercion of a medium (see Acts 5:1–11).

## Chapter 7 Beginning at the End of All Things

1. Democritus, Fragment 230; quoted in Jan N. Bremmer, *Initiation into the Mysteries of the Ancient World* (Boston: de Gruyter, 2014), 1.

2. Mary Beard, "A Complex of Times: No More Sheep on Romulus' Birthday," *Proceedings of the Cambridge Philological Society* 33, no. 213 (1987): 7.

3. Jon Iddeng, "What Is a Graeco-Roman Festival? A Polythetic Approach," in *Greek and Roman Festivals: Content, Meaning, and Practice*, ed. J. Rasmus Brandt and Jon W. Iddeng (Oxford: Oxford University Press, 2012), 11–37: "Through its ritual programme and renewal of the obligations to the gods, the Graeco-Roman festivals in many ways cemented the existing political order as part of the *pax deorum*, commonly with the current political leaders as key celebrants. A festival was about staging power and the existing power structure" (28).

4. Livy writes, "In these latter years wealth has brought avarice in its train, and the unlimited command of pleasure has created in men a passion for ruining themselves and everything else through self-indulgence and licentiousness." Livy, *History of Rome*, ed. Canon Roberts, trans. William Masfen Roberts, History of Rome (Medford, MA: Dutton, 1912), 1.12.

5. Dionysius of Halicarnassus, *Roman Antiquities* 1.6.

6. See Joshua Noble, *Common Property, the Golden Age, and Empire in Acts 2:42–47 and 4:32–35* (London: T&T Clark, 2020).

7. Virgil, *Aeneid* 6.791–3; trans. C. Marvin Pate, *The End of the Age Has Come* (Grand Rapids: Zondervan, 1995), 99.

8. Rabbi Sacks, "Counting Time," May 7, 2015, https://www.rabbisacks.org /archive/counting-time/.

9. Sacks, "Counting Time."

10. Sacks, "Counting Time."

11. See Dan. 11:14; Tobit 14:4–5; 2 Esdras 4:37.

12. See Beard "Complex of Times," 1–15; see also Michael Lipka, *Roman Gods: A Conceptual Approach* (Boston: Brill, 2009), 50.

13. Robert A. Guelich, *Mark 1–8:26*, Word Biblical Commentary 34a (Waco: Word, 1989), 43.

14. Lipka, *Roman Gods*, 49.

15. Also called the "Day of the Lord" (Isa. 13:6, 9; Jer. 46:10; Ezek. 30:3; Joel 1:15; Amos 5:18; 1 Cor. 5:5; 2 Cor. 1:14; 1 Thess. 5:2; 2 Thess. 2:2; 2 Pet. 3:10).

### Chapter 8  A Household of Faith

1. Minucius Felix, *Octavius* 8, in *The Ante-Nicene Fathers*, vol. 4, trans. and ed. Alexander Roberts, James Donaldson, and Arthur Cleveland Coxe (New York: Cosimo, 2007), 177.

2. Minucius Felix, *Octavius* 10, in *The Ante-Nicene Fathers*, vol. 4, trans. and ed. Alexander Roberts, James Donaldson, and Arthur Cleveland Coxe (New York: Cosimo, 2007), 178.

3. Pliny, *Epistles* 10.96, in *Pliny: Letters and Panegyricus*, vol. 2, *Books 8–10*, LCL, trans. B. Radice (Cambridge, MA: Harvard University Press, 1969), 289.

4. *The Works of Philo: Complete and Unabridged*, new updated ed., trans. C. D. Yonge (Peabody, MA: Hendrickson, 1993), 2:462.

5. The Johannine texts tend to express this in terms of "only begotten" Son (KJV: John 1:14, 18; 3:16, 18; 1 John 4:9).

6. See Joseph H. Hellerman, *When the Church Was a Family: Recapturing Jesus' Vision for Authentic Christian Community* (Nashville: B&H Academic, 2009).

7. Roger W. Gehring, *House Church and Mission* (Peabody, MA: Hendrickson, 2004).

8. Warren Carter, *The Roman Empire and the New Testament* (Nashville: Abingdon, 2010), 114; cf. Reta Halteman Finger, *Of Widows and Meals: Communal Meals in the Book of Acts* (Grand Rapids: Eerdmans, 2007), 175.

9. Plutarch, *Quaestiones Convivales* 643; cited in Richard S. Ascough "Communal Meals," in *The Oxford Handbook of Early Christian Ritual*, ed. Ristro Uro, Juliette J. Day, Richard E. DeMaris, and Rikard Roitto (Oxford: Oxford University Press, 2019), 208.

10. Plutarch, *On the Love of Riches* 528B; cited in Ascough, "Communal Meals", 209.

11. See Suetonius, *Augustus* 2.74: "He gave dinner parties constantly and always formally, with great regard to the rank and personality of his guests." In *Lives of the Caesars*, vol. 1, trans. J. C. Rolfe, LCL (Cambridge, MA: Harvard University Press, 1914), 262–63.

### Chapter 9  A Priest-God and a Priestly People

1. AnneMarie Luijendijk, "On and Beyond Duty: Christian Clergy at Oxyrhynchus (c. 250–400)," in *Beyond Priesthood: Religious Entrepreneurs and Innovators in the Imperial Era*, ed. Richard L. Godon, Jörg Rüpke, and Georgia Petridou (New York: de Gruyter, 2017), 103–26. A similar analysis of the texts of the Apostolic Fathers reflects comparable trends, including the importance of bishops and the entire absence of priests; see 1 Clement 42.1, 44.1; see also Beate Dignas, Robert C. T. Parker, and Guy G. Stroumsa, eds., *Priests and Prophets among Pagans, Jews and Christians* (Leuven: Peeters, 2013).

2. Josephus, *Against Apion* 2.108.

3. Mishnah Sukkah 5.7.

4. Robert Kugler, "Priest, Priesthood," in *Eerdmans Dictionary of Early Judaism*, ed. John J. Collins and Daniel C. Harlow (Grand Rapids: Eerdmans, 2010), 1099.

5. Kugler, "Priest, Priesthood," 1099.

6. Kugler, "Priest, Priesthood," 1098.

7. Josephus, *Jewish War* 2.16.2; see Matt 2:4 and 16:21; chief priests are mentioned over fifty times in the Gospels.

8. N. T. Wright, *The New Testament and the People of God* (Minneapolis: Fortress, 2002), 210.

9. See Michael Lipka, *Roman Gods: A Conceptual Approach* (Boston: Brill, 2009), 51–52.

10. Lipka, *Roman Gods*, 51; Mary Beard, John North, and Simon R. F. Price, *Religions of Rome* (Cambridge: Cambridge University Press, 1998), 2:171.

11. Hans-Josef Klauck, *The Religious Context of Early Christianity: A Guide to the Graeco-Roman Religions* (Edinburgh: T&T Clark, 2000), 32.

12. Cicero, *On the Laws* 2.19–22

13. Livy, *History of Rome*, vol. 1, *Books 1–2*, trans. B. O. Foster, LCL (Cambridge, MA: Harvard University Press, 1919), 131.

14. Dionysius of Halicarnassus, *Roman Antiquities* 2.72.

15. The full name of this college is *Quindecimviri sacris faciundis* ("The fifteen performing sacred ceremonies").

16. Allen M. Ward, Fritz M. Heichelheim, and Cedric A. Yeo, *A History of the Roman People*, 6th ed. (New York: Taylor & Francis, 2014), 62; cf. Klauck, *Religious Context of Early Christianity*, 32.

17. Philo, *Dreams* 2.185–189.
18. However, the reality is that many synagogue teachers were also priests, though it was not a requirement for synagogue leadership.
19. Luijendijk, "On and Beyond Duty," 123.

## Chapter 10  Dangerous Contact

1. An older generation of scholarship used the language of "mystery religions," but it is crucial to understand that worshipers in these mystery cults did not reject the state gods. This was a focused devotion, but typically not an exclusive one.
2. Hans-Josef Klauck, *The Religious Context of Early Christianity: A Guide to the Graeco-Roman Religions* (Edinburgh: T&T Clark, 2000), 86.
3. George Heyman, *The Power of Sacrifice: Roman and Christian Discourses in Conflict* (Washington, DC: Catholic University of America Press, 2007), 26.
4. Dionysius of Halicarnassus, *Roman Antiquities* 2.19.3–5.
5. Livy, *History* 39.8–14. Quotations in this paragraph are from Livy, *History of Rome, Book 39*, trans. Rev. Canon Roberts (New York: Dutton, 1912), https://www.perseus.tufts.edu/hopper/text?doc=Perseus:text:1999.02.0026.
6. Livy, *History* 39.8.
7. Livy, *History* 39.8.
8. Livy, *History* 39.13.
9. Livy, *History* 39.13.
10. Aldrete comments: "From a Roman perspective, Christianity initially was just one more strange mystery cult from the East." Gregory S. Aldrete, *Daily Life in the Roman City: Rome, Pompeii, and Ostia* (Westport, CT: Greenwood, 2004), 163.
11. Bruce Metzger, "Considerations of Methodology in the Study of the Mystery Religions and Early Christianity," *Harvard Theological Review* 48, no. 1 (1955): 1–20.
12. Epictetus, *Discourses* 1.20.15. A lot of the material in this section is found in Willis P. DeBoer, *The Imitation of Paul: An Exegetical Study* (Eugene, OR: Wipf & Stock, 2016), 28–29.
13. Epictetus, *Discourses* 3.19.27; quoted in DeBoer, *Imitation of Paul*, 28.
14. Epictetus *Discourses* 2.14.13; quoted in DeBoer, *Imitation of Paul*, 29.
15. Seneca, *Epistles* 92.27; cf. Plutarch, *Moralia* 1.5.
16. Seneca, *Epistles* 92.27.
17. See Musonius Rufus, Lecture 27.
18. G. K. Beale, *We Become What We Worship: A Biblical Theology of Idolatry* (Downers Grove, IL: IVP Academic, 2008).
19. See David A. deSilva, *Honor, Patronage, Kinship, and Purity: Unlocking New Testament Culture*, 2nd ed. (Downers Grove, IL: IVP Academic, 2022), 211–12.
20. See Kent L. Yinger, *God and Human Wholeness: Perfection in Biblical and Theological Tradition* (Eugene, OR: Cascade Books, 2019).

21. Some ancient writers defended the mysteries as morally formative. See the discussion in Bruce W. Longenecker, *In Stone and Story: Early Christianity in the Roman World* (Grand Rapids: Baker Academic, 2020), 93–94.

### Chapter 11 To Treat All as Equal

1. See Pamela Johnston, "'All Strangers and Beggars Are from Zeus': Early Greek Views of Hospitality," *Pacific Journal* 13 (2018): 106.

2. Pliny, *The Letters of the Younger Pliny* 9.5; trans. J. D. Lewis (London: Kegan Paul, 1890), 293.

3. Jerry Toner, *The Roman Guide to Slave Management: A Treatise by Nobleman Marcus Sidonious Falx* (New York: Overlook, 2014), 131.

4. Toner, *Roman Guide to Slave Management*, 132.

5. Toner, *Roman Guide to Slave Management*, 134–35.

6. Fanny Dolansky, "Celebrating the Saturnalia: Religious Ritual and Roman Domestic Life," in *A Companion to Families in the Greek and Roman Worlds*, ed. Beryl Rawson (West Sussex, UK: Wiley-Blackwell, 2011), 488–503.

7. Catullus *Poem* 14.15; from *The Complete Poetry of Catullus*, trans. D. Mulroy (Madison: University of Wisconsin Press, 2002), lvii.

8. Tacitus, *Annals* 13.15.

9. Pliny, *Letters* 2.17.24.

10. Horace, *Satires* 2.7; Martial, *Epigrams* 14.79.

11. Solinus, *Collection of Memorable Things* 1.35.

12. Historia Augusta, *Life of Verus* 7.5.

13. Seneca, *Epistles* 47.

14. Lucian, *Saturnalia* 4.

15. Dolansky, "Celebrating the Saturnalia," 499.

16. See also Polycarp, *Epistle to the Philippians* 6.1.

### Chapter 12 The Christians Were Not Perfect

1. Stephen E. Young proposes that Philemon offering Onesimus his freedom would be taken for granted. *Our Brother Beloved: Purpose and Community in Paul's Letter to Philemon* (Waco: Baylor University Press, 2021).

2. As explained by Josephus, *Jewish Antiquities* 18.21.

3. See Ignatius, *To Polycarp* 4.3; Didache 4.10. For an academic analysis, see Mary E. Sommar, *The Slaves of the Churches: A History* (Oxford: Oxford University Press, 2020), 38–106.

4. For a robust discussion of this, see Luke Timothy Johnson, "The New Testament's Anti-Jewish Slander and the Conventions of Ancient Polemic," *Journal of Biblical Literature* 108, no. 3 (1989): 419–41.

5. See my work in *1–2 Thessalonians*, Zondervan Critical Introductions to the New Testament (Grand Rapids: Zondervan Academic, 2019).